Jack A. Zucker

Sheets of Sound
Vol II

Intermediate and Advanced Studies

Version 1.0.0.0

Web: *http://www.sheetsofsound.net*
Email: *jaz@sheetsofsound.net*

Copyright © 2006 by Jack A. Zucker
All rights reserved

Jack A. Zucker
www.SheetsOfSound.net

Introduction

Sheets of Sound for Guitar Vol II is a natural evolution of the **Sheets of Sound Vol I**. It continues along much of the same harmonic and rhythmic path while putting more emphasis on *real world* examples and delving into asymetrical, odd-meter groupings and artist studies. The artist studies are inspired by Pat Metheny, George Benson, Frank Gambale, Pat Martino and John Coltrane and are very exciting to learn and perform.

Traditionally, jazz guitarists have been taught to play melodies across the neck of the instrument while staying in a single left hand position and alternating between *upstrokes* and *downstrokes* with the plectrum. This traditional approach to the instrument creates a percussive effect which allows the instrument to generate a very strong pulse or *swing* and is part of its unique flavor. However, the traditional technique is not necessarily conducive to playing the instrument with the explosive bursts of notes that are possible on the wind instruments such as saxophone or trumpet.

I've spent many years trying to emulate horn players such as Charlie Parker, Dizzy Gillespie, John Coltrane and Mike Brecker. However, It seemed that no matter how much I practiced, I could not attain the smooth flowing legato feel that I was after.

As I explored the issue in greater depth, I realized that it had to do with momentum. A horn player creates *momentum* by blowing a single stream of air and fingering multiple notes. This *momentum* was never more prominant than in the '60s when John Coltrane rose to prominence. Coltrane pioneered a technique of playing a considerable amount of notes in a small amount of time (**Fig. 1**). This flurry of notes washed over the listener in such a way as to be described as *Sheets of Sound*.

Fig. 1

This technique is difficult for guitarists to emulate because of the physical limitations of the instrument as well as the way we were taught to play in horizontally across the fingerboard with strict alternate picking. Overcoming these restrictions will unlock your playing and allow you to take the next step beyond the limitations of your current technique.

Note: **THIS BOOK IS NOT ABOUT SWEEP PICKING**. It is about using the entire instrument horizontally and vertically as well as unlocking your mind to its possibilities. The techniques described herein are applicable to pick, fingers, hybrid and any other type of right hand approach.

I hope you have as much fun learning this material as I've had writing it.

Keep on pickin',

Jack A. Zucker

Acknowledgements

Sy Zucker — It is most difficult to thank you because you have given me so many gifts. You instilled upon me a sense of commitment to the art and craft of music. You are also the single most sincere, genuine and generous person I have ever known. I will spend the rest of my life trying to live up to your legacy.

My sister Melanie — Thanks for being there when I needed you.

Sandra Lester — Thanks for your kindness and patience. Your love and support is my inspiration in life and my music.

Jo Zucker, Mike Imlay, Fanny and Somy Benherzal, whose spirits radiate from these pages.

Ed DeGenaro (www.eddegenaro.com) for his incredible virtuosity and guidance about the music business.

John Coltrane, Charlie Parker, George Benson, Rodney Jones, Dave Liebman, Michael Brecker, Herbie Hancock, Elvin Jones, Tony Williams, Shawn Lane, Allen Holdsworth, McCoy Tyner, Louis Johnson, Victor Wooten — The inspiration for this work.

Janet Kuhn, Claudio Ballestero, Jim Roberts, Tom & Trish Walters, Gilbert Harmon, Scott Lerner, Paul Horn and Maceo Noisette, whose positive attitude towards life and music have continually renewed my spirit.

Jon Sterngold (www.lifepathguide.com) for the advice and guidance I needed to stay healthy, mentally and physically.

Tobias Giesen at TGTools (www.tgtools.com) for his Finale® Plug-in Tools. (Finale® is a registered trademark of Code Music Technologies)

John, Larry and Gary at Euphonics Audio (www.euphonicaudio.com) for providing bass amps and bass cabinets which are supreme.

AcousticImg (www.acousticimg.com) for making a portable and wonderful sounding guitar amp.

THD (www.thdamps.com) for supplying the best sounding guitar cabinets and attenuators you can buy.

Dimarzio (www.dimarzio.com) for making pickups that prove you don't have to pay boutique prices to have boutique tone.

D'Addario (www.daddario.com) for supplying strings and accessories.

Jim Soloway (www.jimsoloway.com) for having the courage to make a *different* guitar.

Alf Hermida (www.hermidaaudio.com) for supplying the Zendrive.

Pete Skjold (www.skjolddesign.com) for making the best bass in the universe.

And finally, thanks to Andrew and Jeremy for being the greatest gift of all. This book is dedicated to you both.

Legend

Symbol	Description
⊓	*downstroke*
V	*upstroke*
1-4	Left hand fingers
p	Pick
i	Index finger (not used with pick)
m	Middle finger
a	Ring finger
c	Little finger
♪ ♪	*Hammer-on* or *pull-off*
x@y	column@row, representing table cell locations

Arpeggio Scales

Exercise 1 - *4 String Arpeggio Scale*

The arpeggio scale is just what it sounds like - A combination of a scale and an arpeggio. It combines arpeggios and diatonics. It is a very efficient model for outlining chords and extensions.

The example is notated in septuplets. Like many of the exercises in the book, you can choose to play it as written with 7 notes to the bar or you can use the barlines as guidelines and simply play the exercise as a waterfall of notes.

The following example shows several common chord types with examples of arpeggio scales over them. Don't forget to apply these techniques up and down the neck as well as throughout all string combinations.

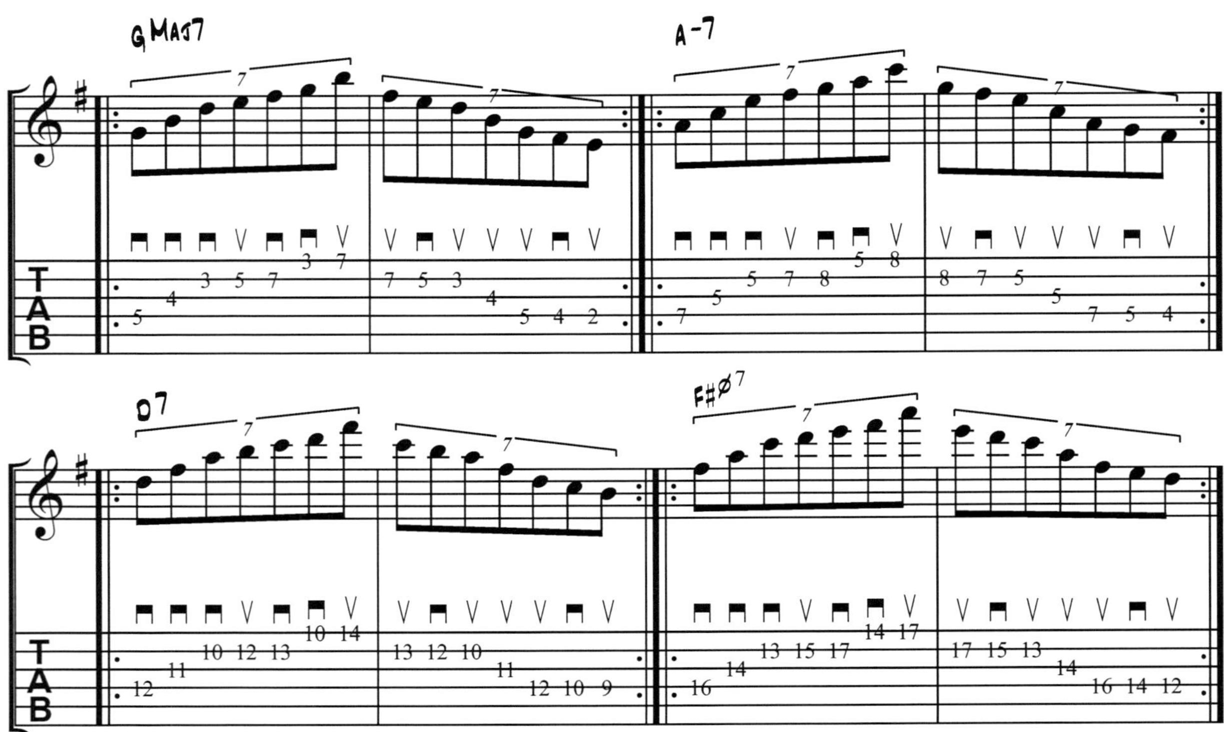

Real World Example: This example uses an Ab diminished arpeggio-scale over the G7 before resolving to the CMaj7 chord.

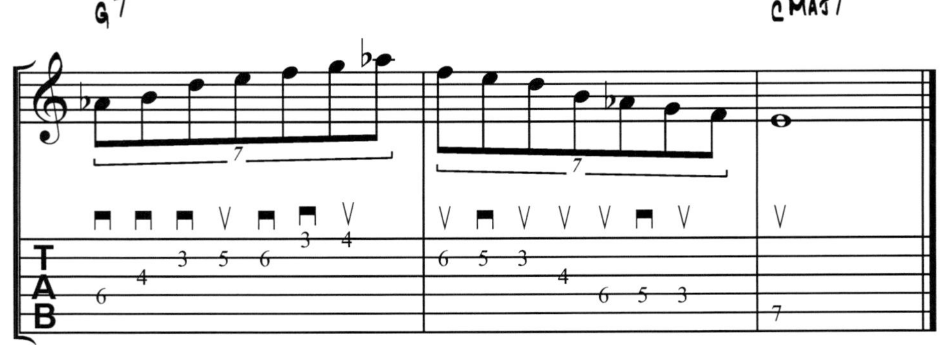

Exercise 2 - *5 String Arpeggio Scale*

Here's a 5 string arpeggio scale utilizing a C melodic minor tonality. Following are 4 inversions of this arpeggio scale that I find interesting. The music is notated as 18 notes per measure but it's easier to play these sequences as a waterfall of notes. Don't worry about exact placement of downbeats and barlines. Eventually, you will feel these patterns and the rhythmic freedom will become a part of your creative arsenal.

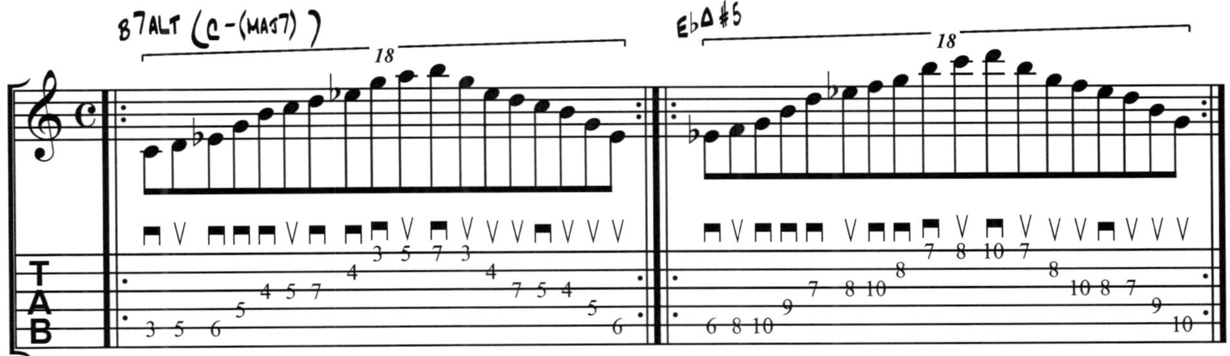

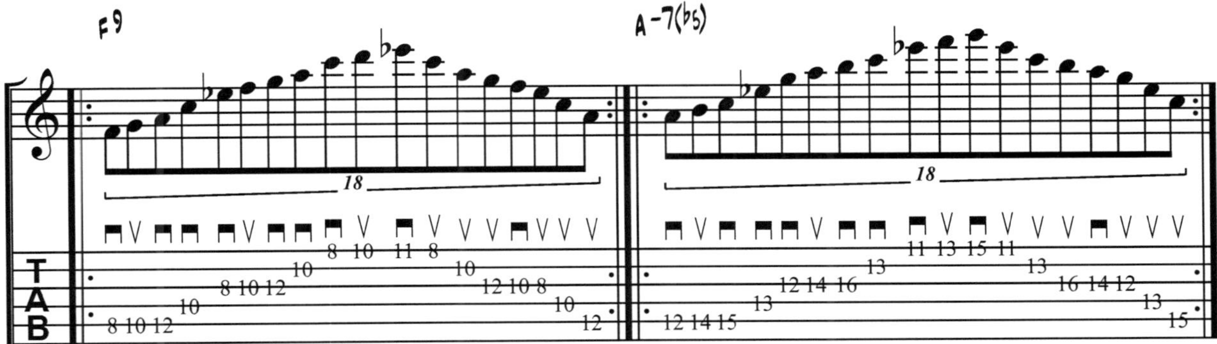

Real World Example: This example uses F melodic minor over the Dm7b5 chord, Ab melodic minor over the G7 chord and A melodic minor over the Cmaj7 chord (yielding the maj7#5 tonality)

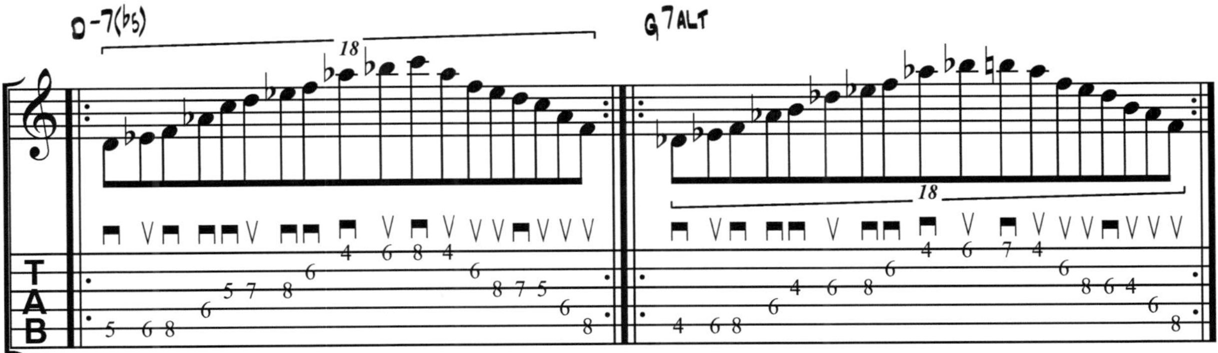

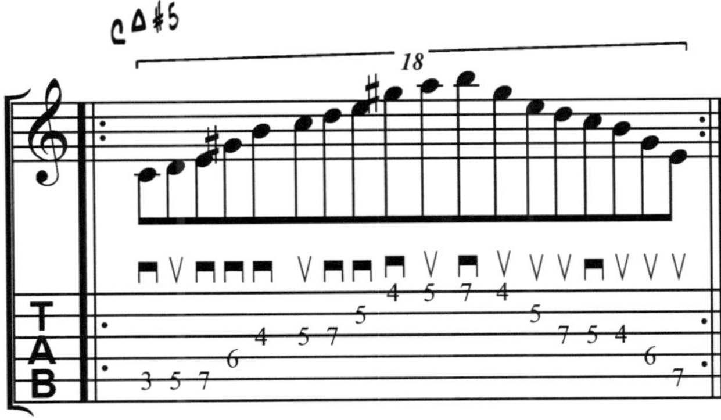

Exercise 3 - 6 String Arpeggio Scale

Here's the 6 string version of the arpeggio scale, this time notated as untuplets (11/8). I suggest playing these as waterfalls of notes as opposed to trying to count them out exactly at when first practicing them. I have not written out every mode of this arpeggio scale so make sure you work this out in all positions and other tonalities such as melodic minor, harmonic minor, diminished, etc.

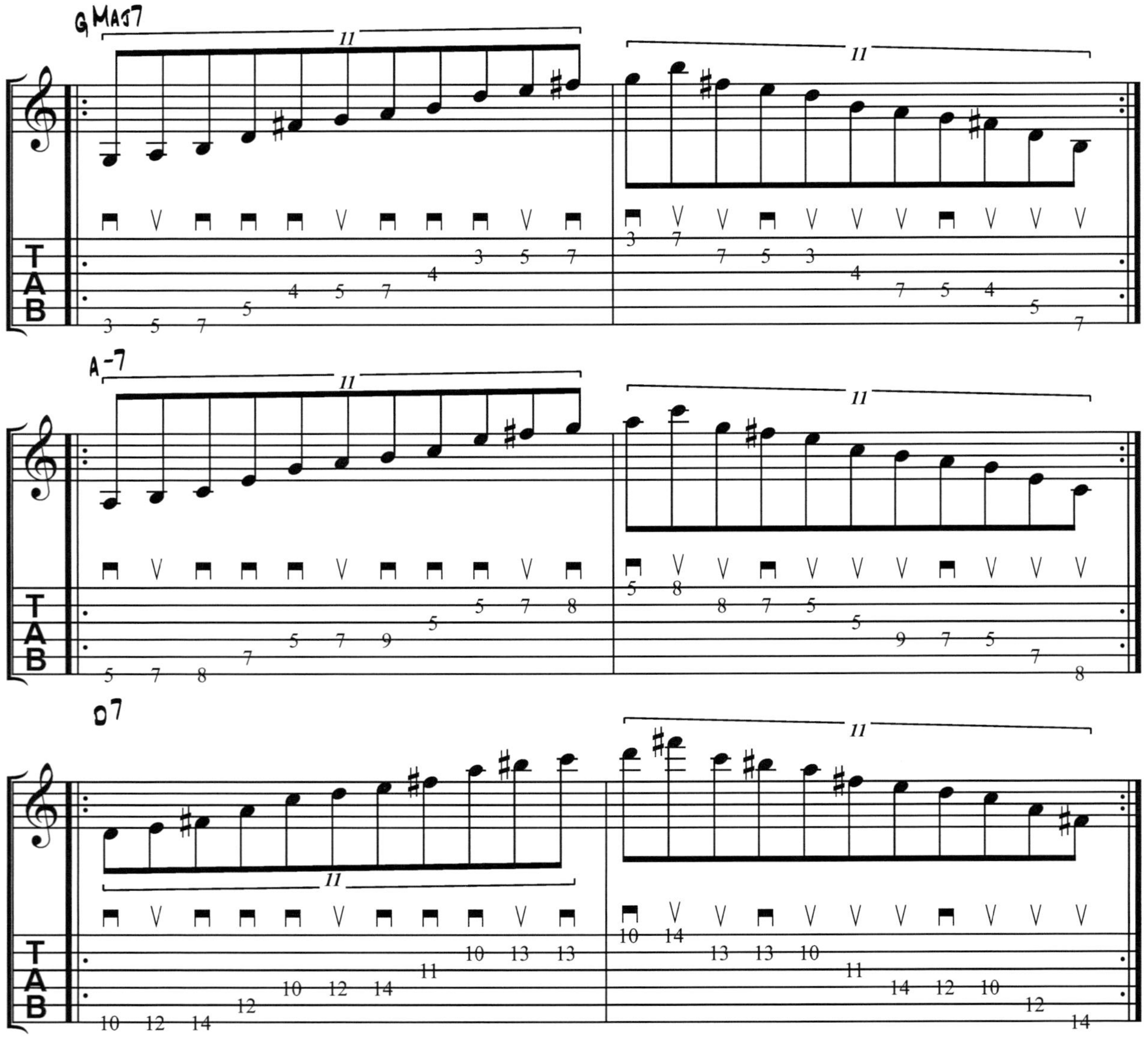

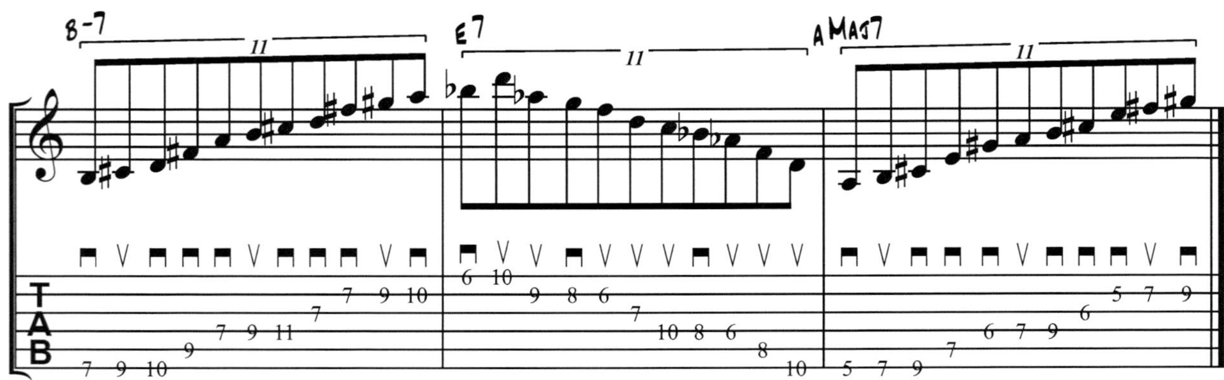

Real World Example: This example uses B Dorian over the B-7 chord, Bb7 (F Melodic minor) over the E7 chord and A Ionian over the Amaj7 chord.

Exercise 4 - *Arpeggio Scale w/4ths*

This exercise combines an arpeggio scale with an enharmonic 4ths phrase at the beginning of each line. The 4ths give the line a modern sound reminiscent of Chick Corea or Frank Gambale.

The notated chords apply to the body of the arpeggio but the principal of diatonic synonyms apply. You can use these lines against any diatonic chord in the key of F. These lines sound particularly good over the ii (G-7) or the iv (BbMaj7) chord.

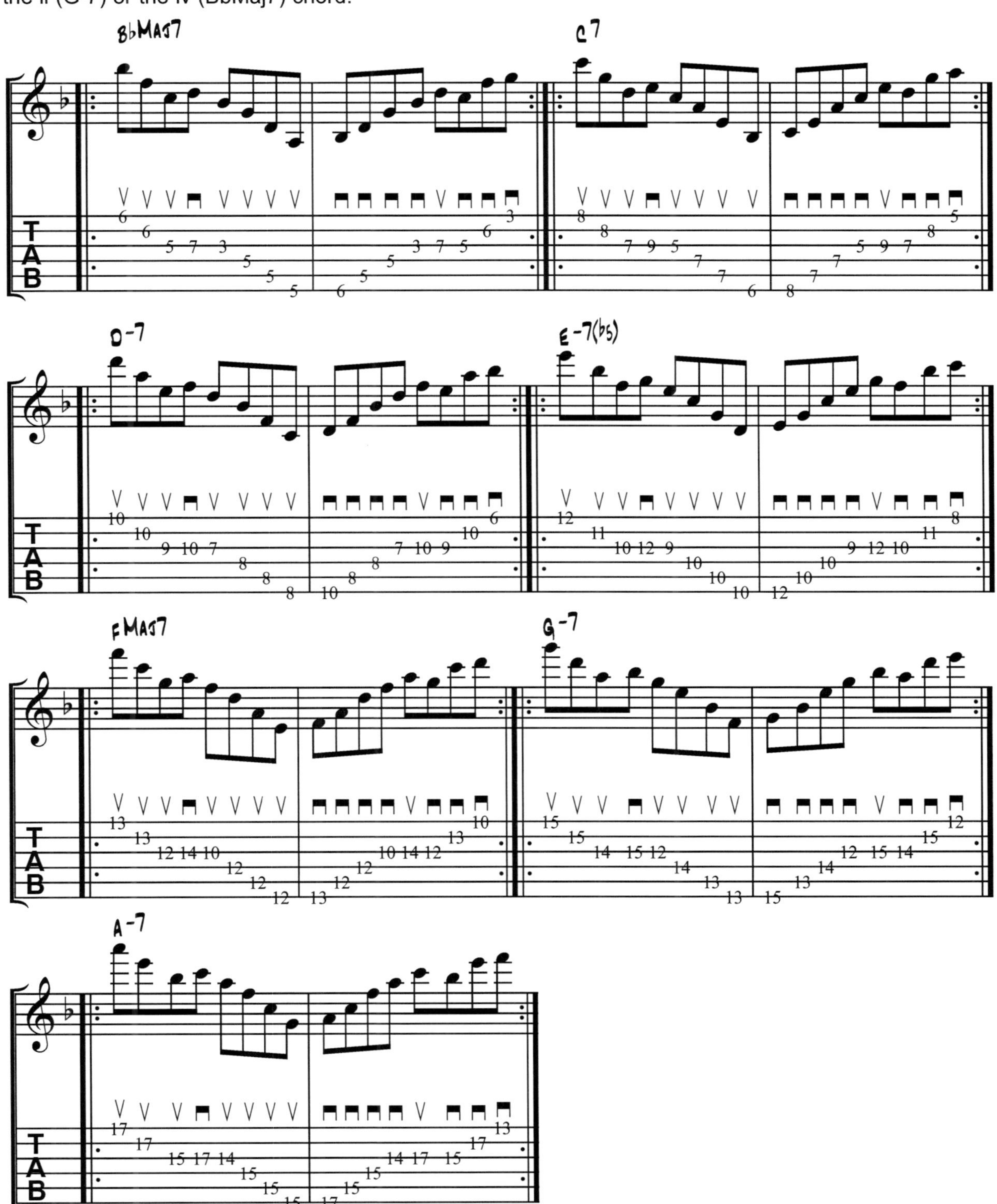

Exercise 5 - *Miscellaneous Dominant Arpeggio Scales*

5.1

The wholetone arpeggio scale is great, easy to play and can be used in any inversion. In the following example, though notated with A7#5, the line is equally at home with A7, B7, C#7, D#7, F7 and G7.

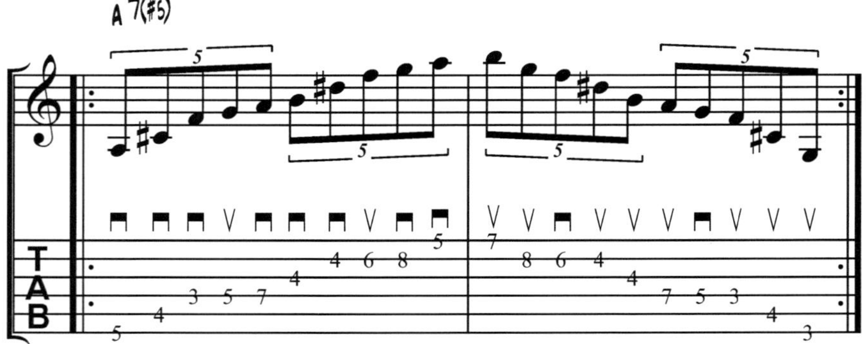

5.2

Another wholetone arpeggio scale. This time a 5 string version in 7 over 8.

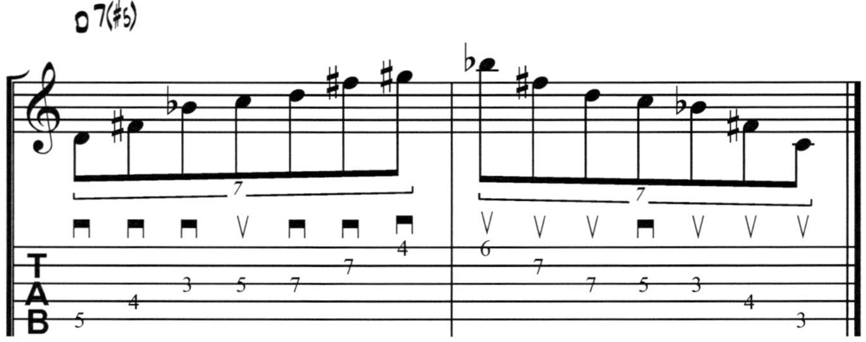

5.3

Here are two inversions of a diminished arpeggio scale. Being symetrical, you can move this up the neck in minor 3rds or play the two inversions in a 1/2 step, whole step pattern.

5.4

Here's the 2nd inversion of the diminished arpeggio scale.

5.5

Here's a melodic minor based example based on the Bb Melodic minor over the A7 chord. This one generates an A7Alt chord.

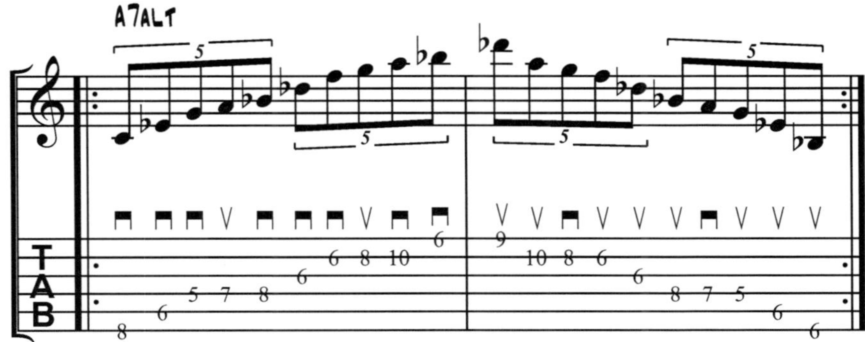

5.6

And another melodic minor based example. This time based on the G Melodic minor over the A7 chord. This creates an A13b9Sus chord.

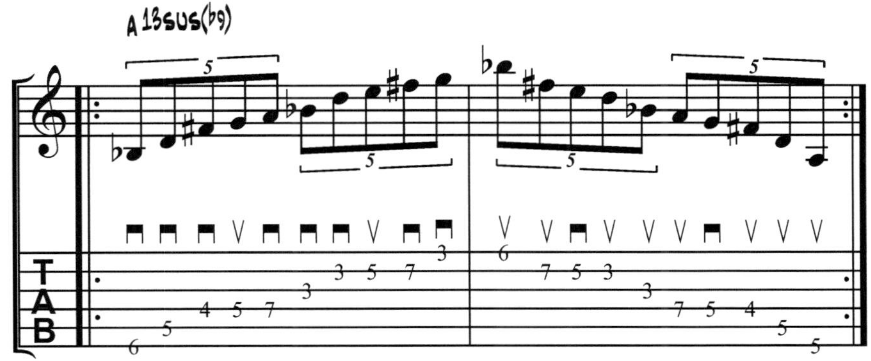

Friends

Ed DeGenaro - www.EdDeGenaro.com

Rodney Jones - www.RodneyJones.com

Diatonic / Intervallic Designs

Exercise 6 - Basic Waterfall Pattern

This is what I call the basic waterfall pattern. I call it this because when played properly, the notes wash over you like a waterfall. Many patterns in the book are based on the concepts of this line. Though this exercise is shown over a G-(maj7) chord and is based on G Melodic minor, the line may be played over a playing G-7, C7, etc.

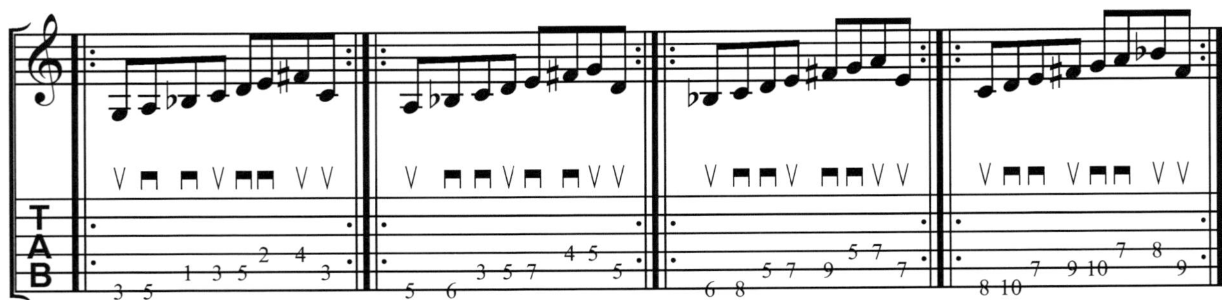

Real World Example: I'm using a dorian based variation over the A-7 chord, a superlocrian (melodic minor off the b9 over the D7 and Lydian off the G.

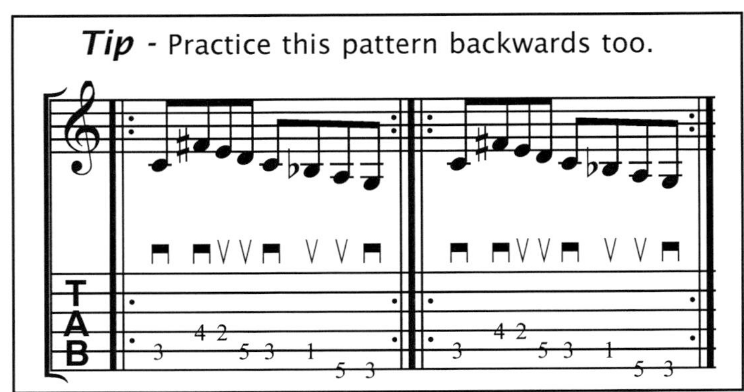

Exercise 7 - 7 over 8 Forced Swept Waterfall

Here's an example of a basic waterfall. This example is a bit unusual in that it utilizes a technique called forced sweeping where the normal sweep pattern is interrupted by an alternate picked pattern. At first this may feel somewhat awkward but it's an important and useful technique to master. You will see this type of device elsewhere in the book.

The break in the sweep pattern occurs between the 5th and 6th notes of the pattern. The arrows denote the break in the sweep pattern.

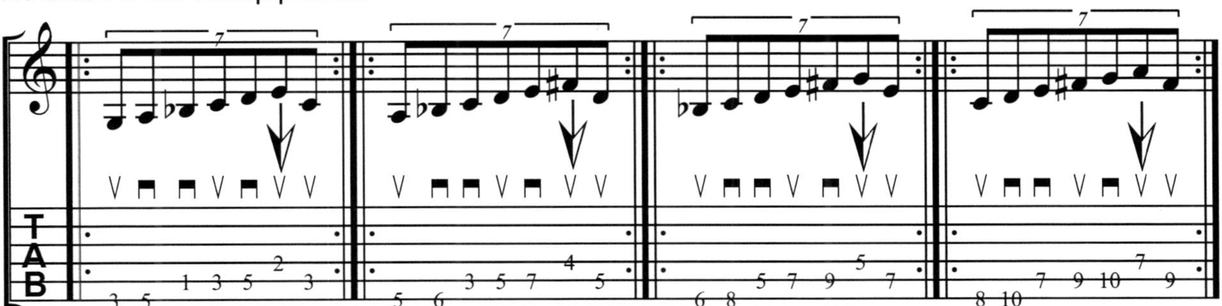

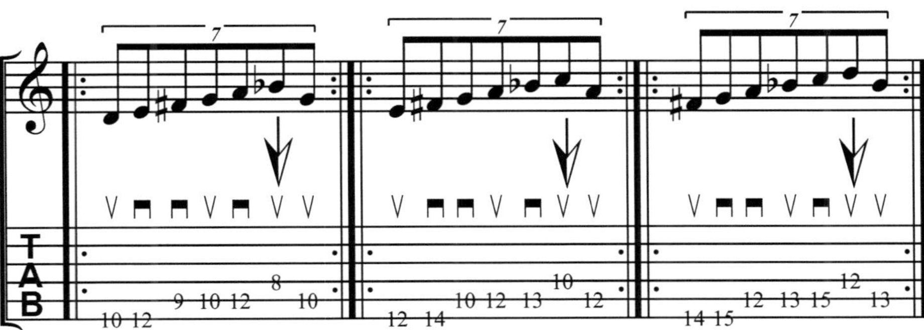

Here's a variation of the original pattern. This time we are forcing a downstroke between the last and the first note of the pattern. (The arrows are omitted in this example)

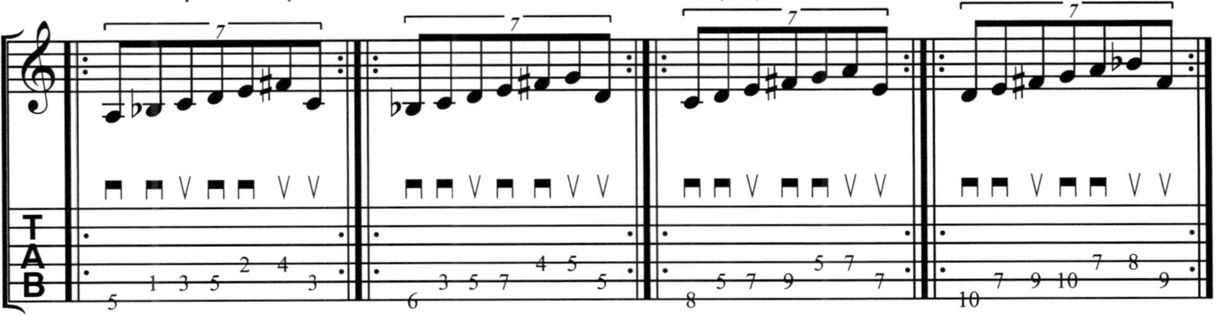

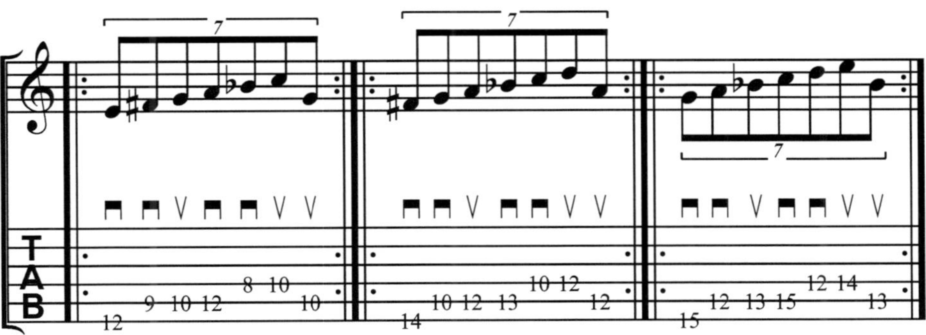

Exercise 8 - Basic 7 over 8 Waterfall Horizontally Extended

This pattern is a variation of the previous waterfall. In this variation the pattern is extended diatonically across the neck of the guitar. To faciliate the waterfall feel, it's played in a 7 over 8 rhythm. It's a beautiful and horn-like way to get from one place to another on the instrument.

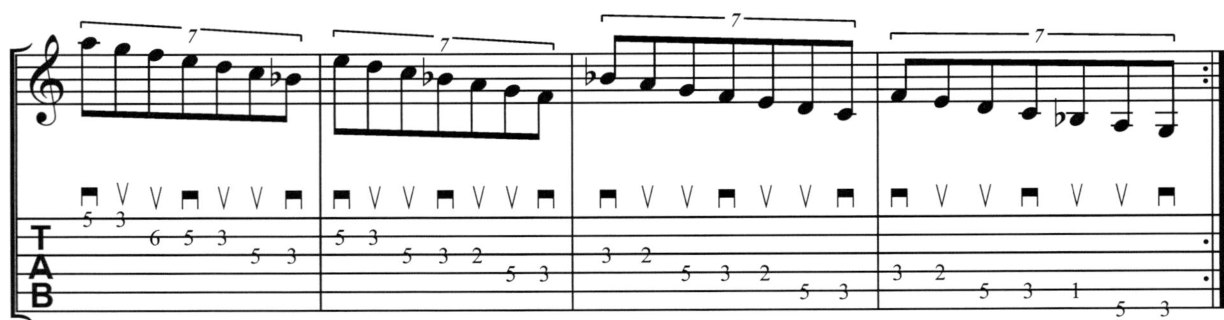

Real World Example: I'm using a Dorian based example over the A-7, a Super Locrian (Melodic Minor off the b9) over the D7 and a G lydian over the GMaj7.

Exercise 9 - 7 over 8 Diminished Waterfall Pattern Horizontally Extended

Here's another 7 over 8 waterfall pattern, this time applied to the diminished scale.

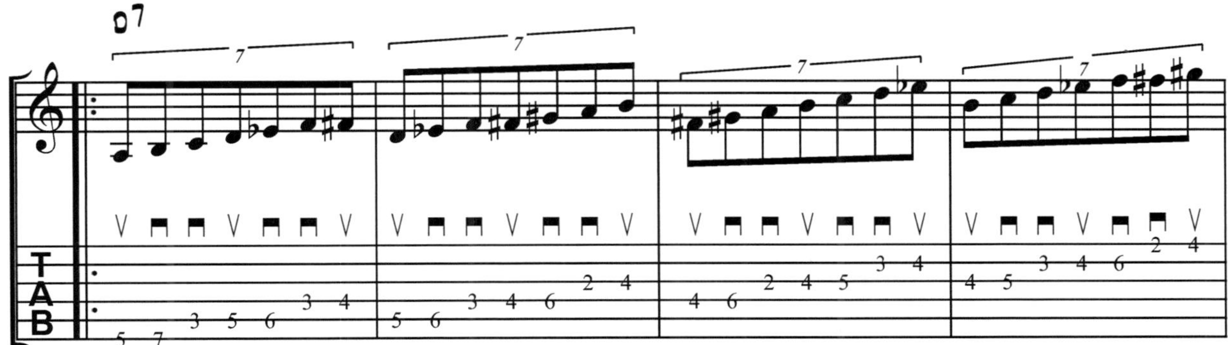

Here's the other inversion of this pattern. Since we're working with the semetrical diminished scale, there are only two modes of the scale to learn.

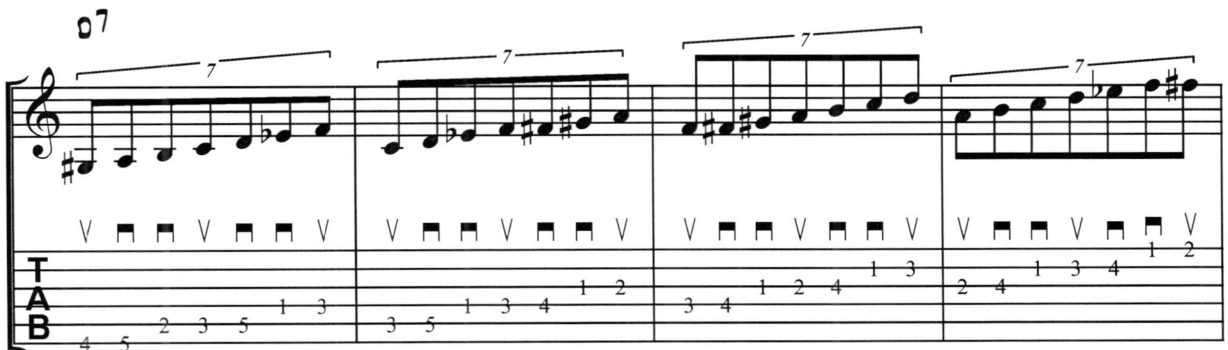

Real World Example: Here's a typical jazz turnaround (Iii-vi-ii-v) using dom7 chords for each chord of the turnaround. We're using the first inversion of this pattern against each of the chords in the turnaround before resolving to the GMaj7 chord.

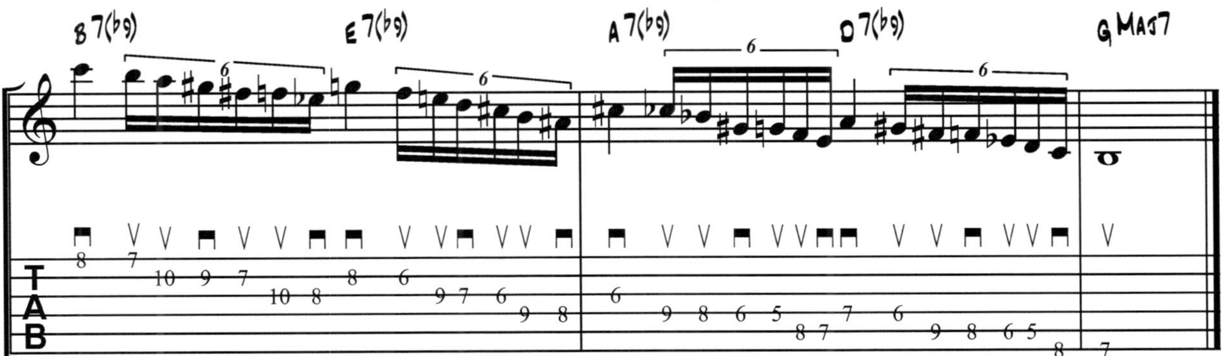

Exercise 10 - 7 over 8 Wholetone Waterfall Pattern Horizontally Extended

Another 7 over 8 waterfall. This time utilizing the wholetone scale. Each measure moves up an augmented 4th. You can use this over any Dom7#5 who's root is in the scale.

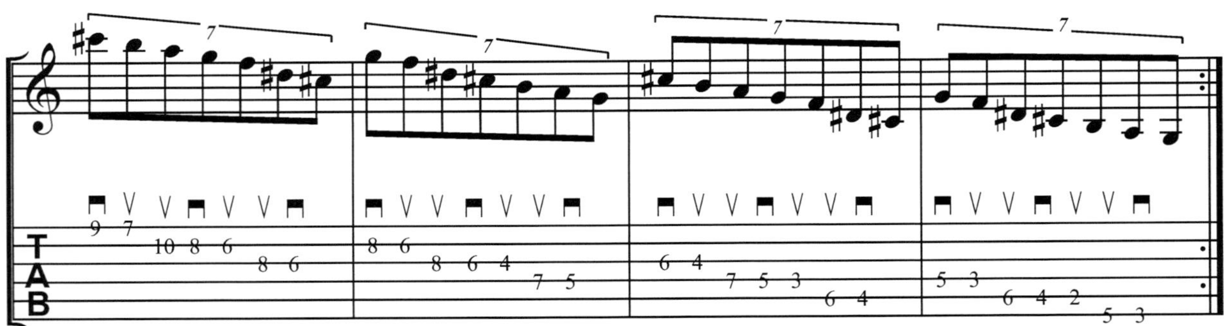

Real World Example: This example utilizes A dorian for the A-7 and D wholetone for the D7 chord.

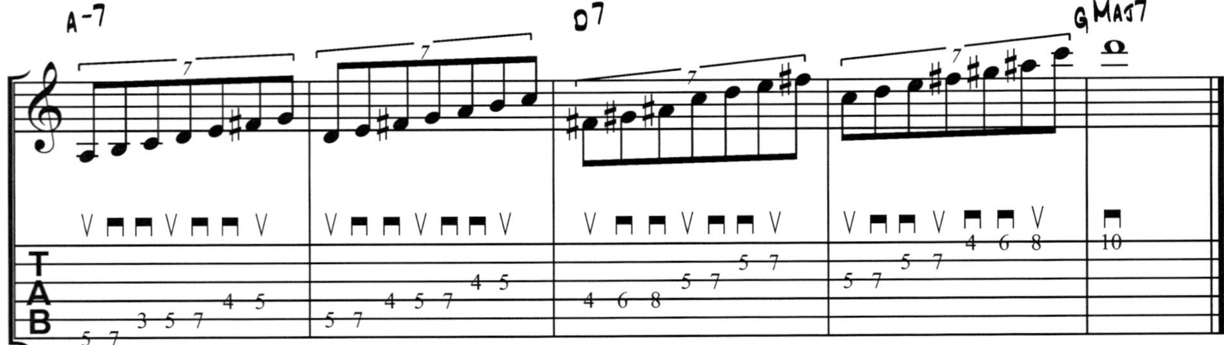

Exercise 11 - 5 over 4 Breckerism

In terms of horn-like phrasing, one of the most important things for a guitarist to develop is the ability to play odd groupings of notes against a polymetric subdivision. In this case, we are playing 10 8th notes over a 4/4 measure. One way to feel this when you are first starting out is to play it as if it were all 8th notes but tap your foot at the beginning of each 5 note grouping. You will eventually begin to feel the 5 over 4 feel.

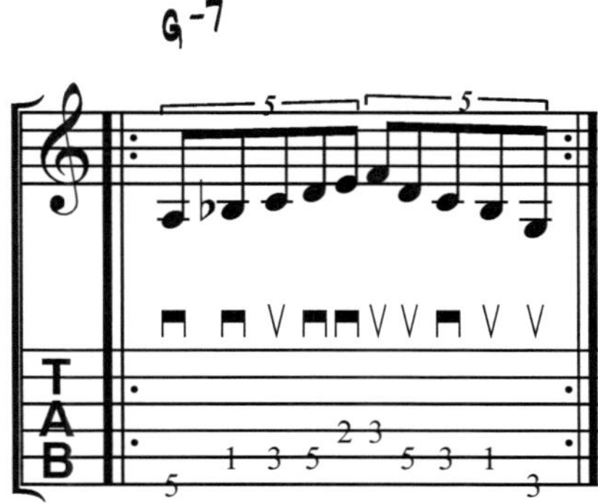

When you are comfortable with this line, a slight variation is to move it up the fretboard diatonically.

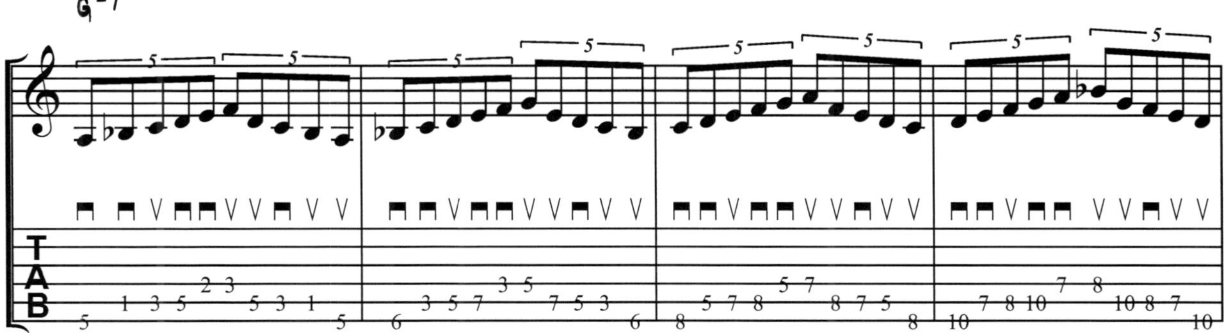

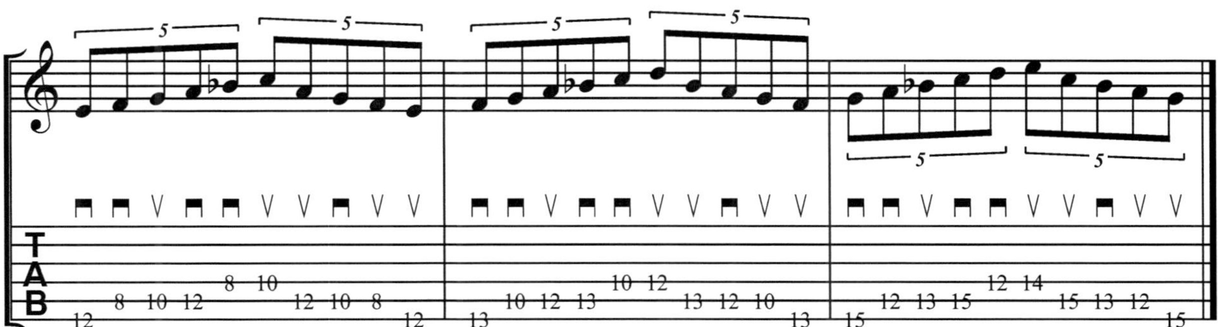

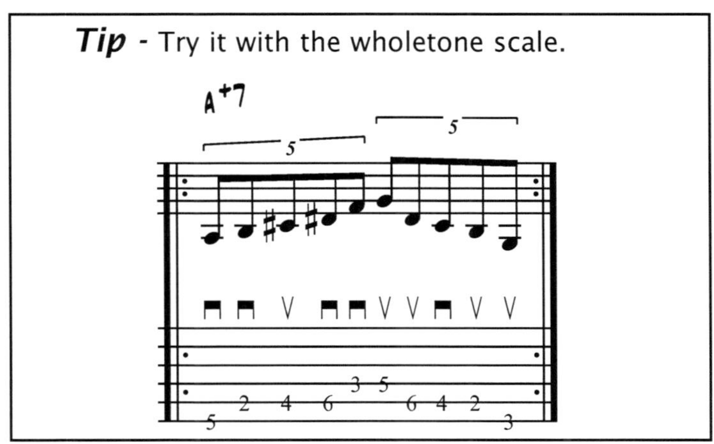

Exercise 12 - Basic 13 over 8 Waterfall

This pattern is simpler than it looks. It's a basic scalar 13 over 8 waterfall. I would advise playing it as a flowing waterfall of notes instead of attempting to subdivide 13 beats per measure. It's an endless pattern in that it can be repeated due to it's symetry. Make sure to transpose to all positions and modes.

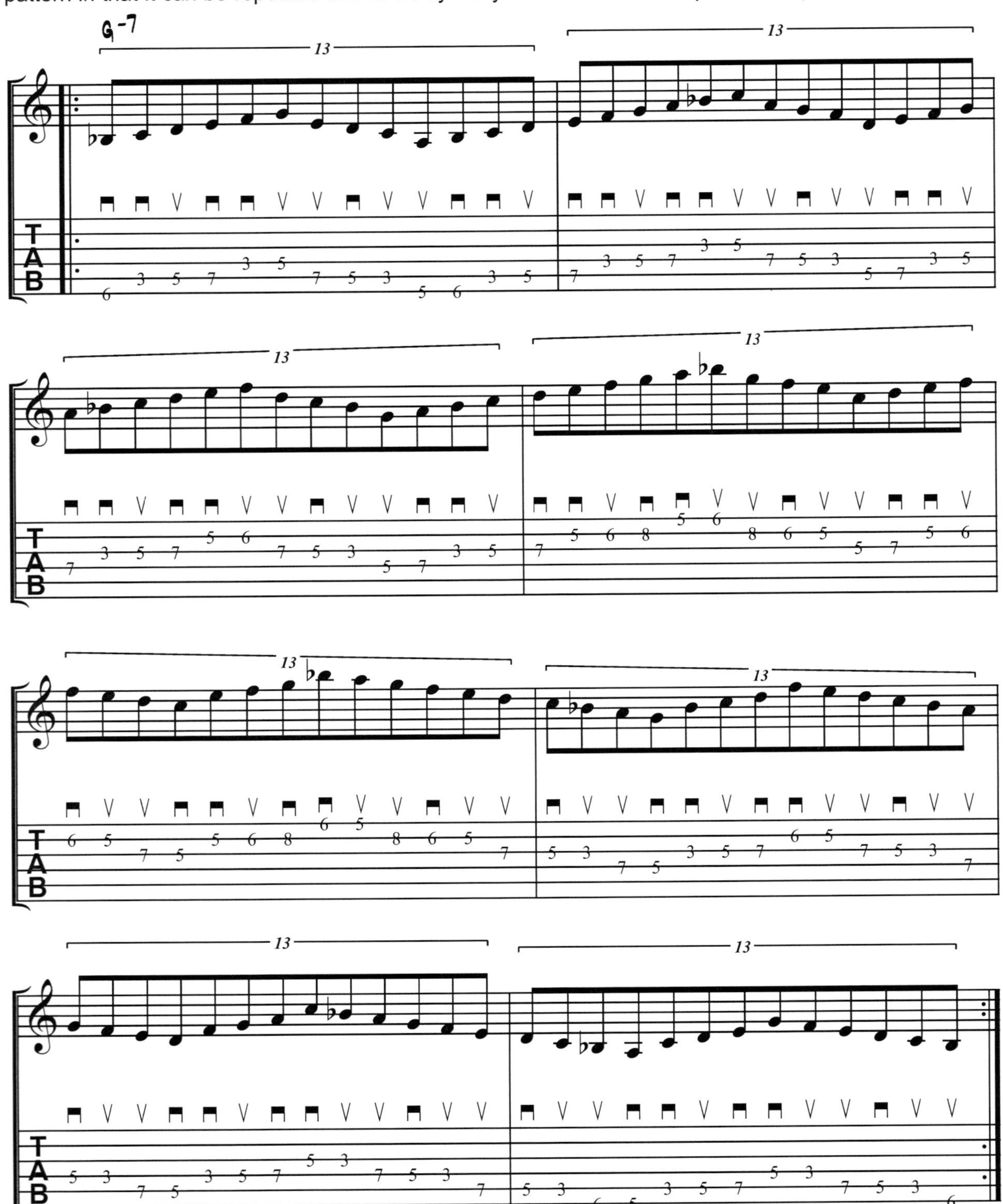

Exercise 13 - 13 over 8 Wholetone Waterfall

Here's the 13 over 8 waterfall applied to the wholetone scale. In addition to 7th chords these can also be used over minor chords. For example, AbmMaj7

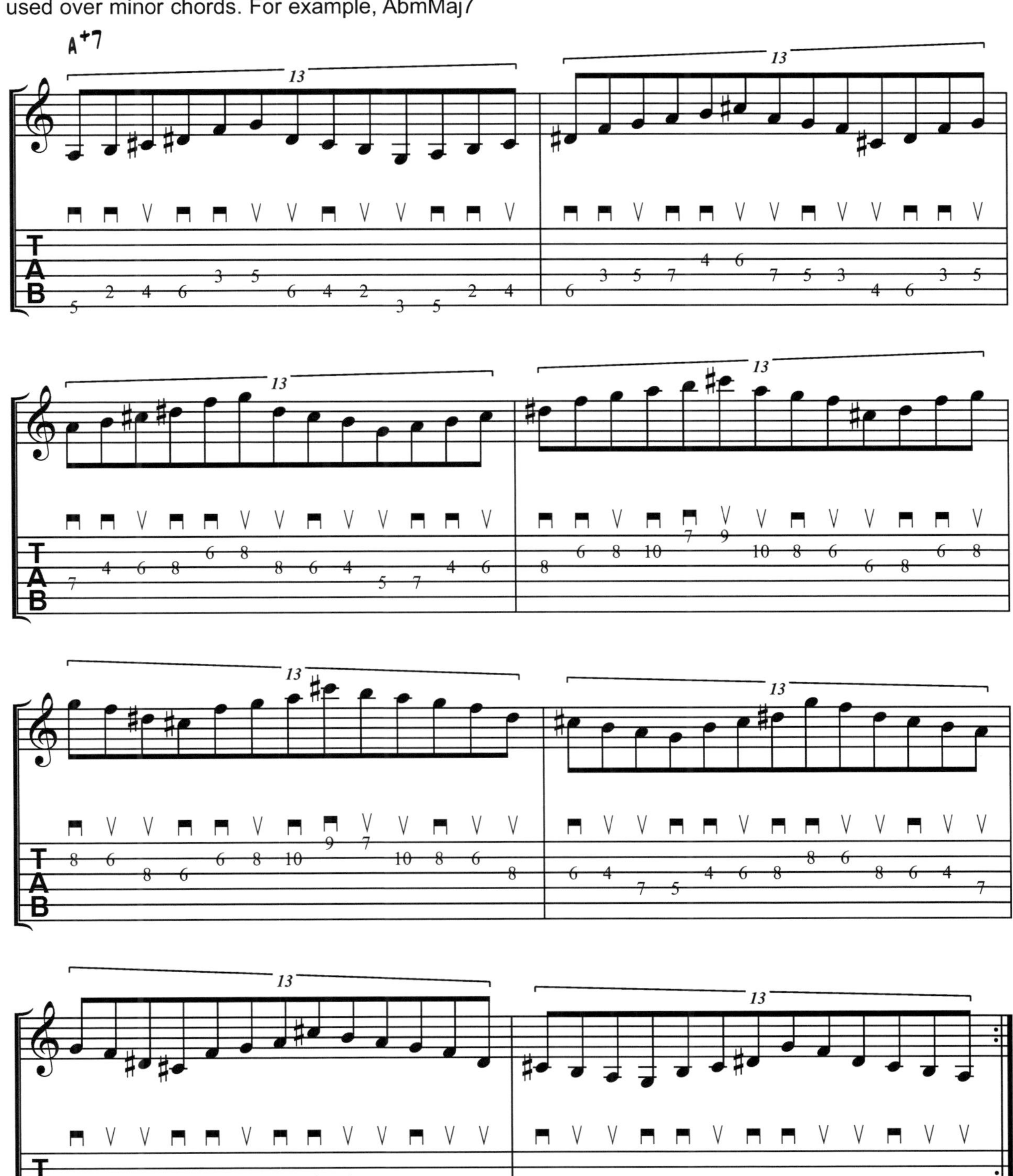

Exercise 14 - 5 over 4 + 13 over 8 Waterfall

This line is based on the 5 over 4 Breckerism but combines that line with 13 over 8 along with moving the line across the fingerboard.

Before you begin panicking about playing it rigidly as indicated, I suggest you ignore the bar lines and play it as a flowing series of notes. This is a great etude and evokes a Coltrane or Holdsworth type of feeling.

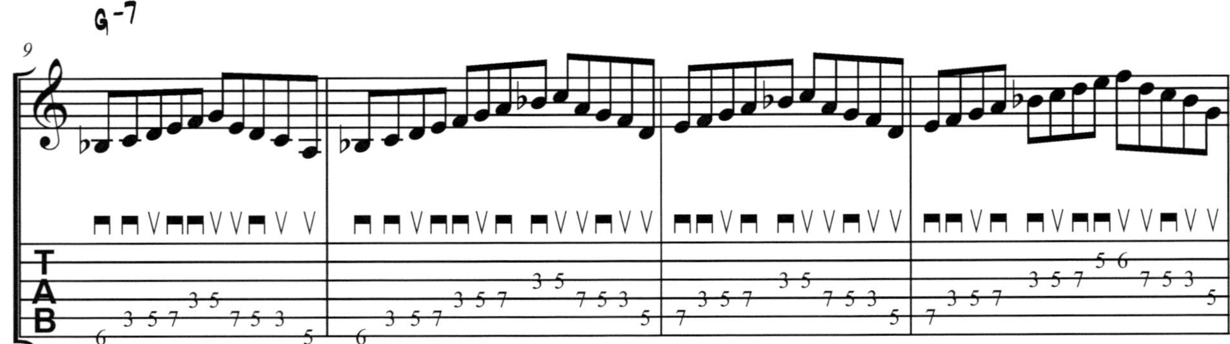

Exercise 15 - Tyner Diatonic and 4th Sweep

Exercise is very interesting and simple. It combines a diatonic sequence followed by 9th chord arpeggio and then a 4th triad. The chords notated are for analysis purposes.

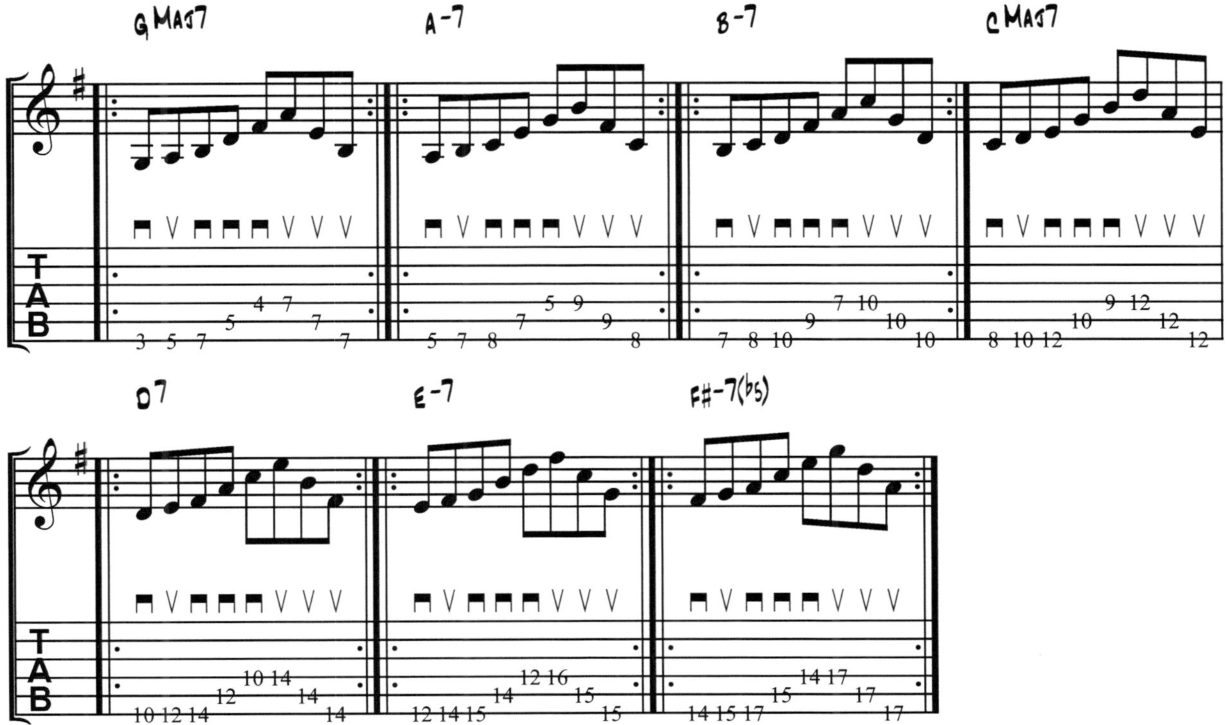

Real World Example: This example demonstrates the pattern over a ii V I chord progression. Notice the usage of Eb Melodic Minor over the D7 and G Lydian over the GMaj7 chord.

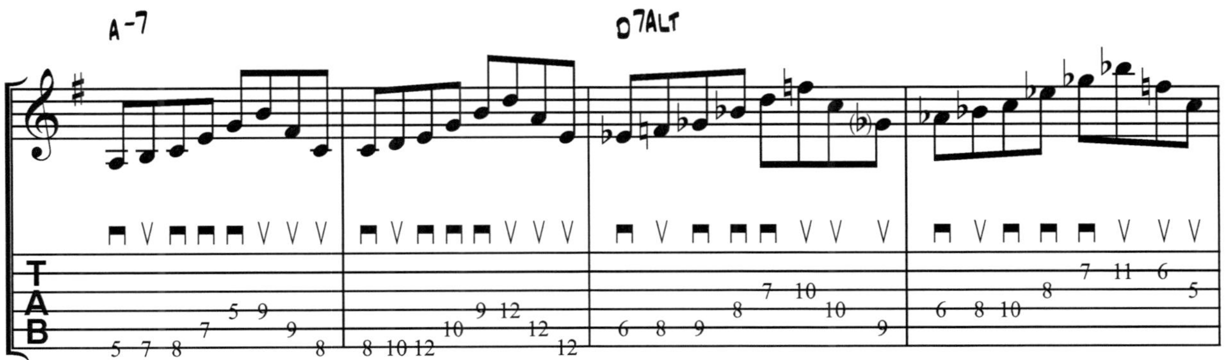

Exercise 16 - Repeated Note Patterns

The first exercise is a septuplet based exercise utilizing repeated notes. You can either play this as a polyrhythmic device (7 or 4) or as 8th notes with accents every 7 notes. Either way, it's a very cool and percussive sounding device. It's someone dissonant in that it's based on a guitaristic fingering pattern as opposed to a melodic device but works! It's also a great technical exercise.

Make sure you practice all these exercises in all modes, positions and backwards too.

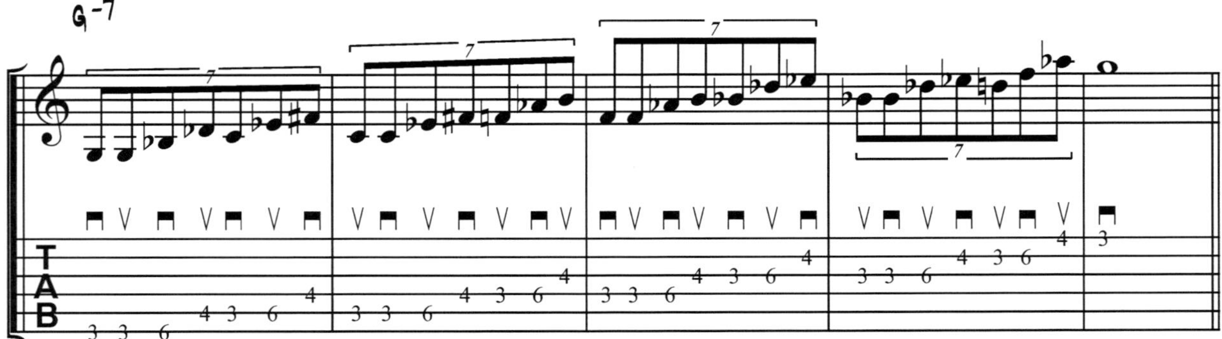

Here's another example based on the pentatonic scale so it sounds more inside.

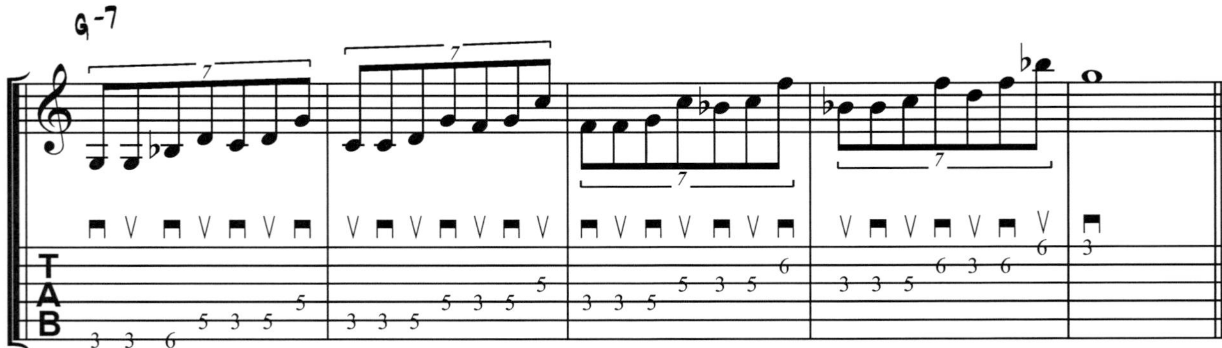

This next example of this technique utilizes a diatonic approach. This particular technique has many applications as you can see!

Exercise 17 - Swept Dectuplet Repeated note pattern

This is one of the most fascinating patterns in the book. It reminds me of something you'd hear Scott Henderson or Mike Brecker play. The sweep picking gives it a waterfall type of sound which allows it to flow over the background rhythm very smoothly. Thought it's notated as 10 over 8, it can be played out of time as well.

Chords are not notated though it's all diatonic to the key of G. This line would sound excellent over an Am7 fusion vamp for example.

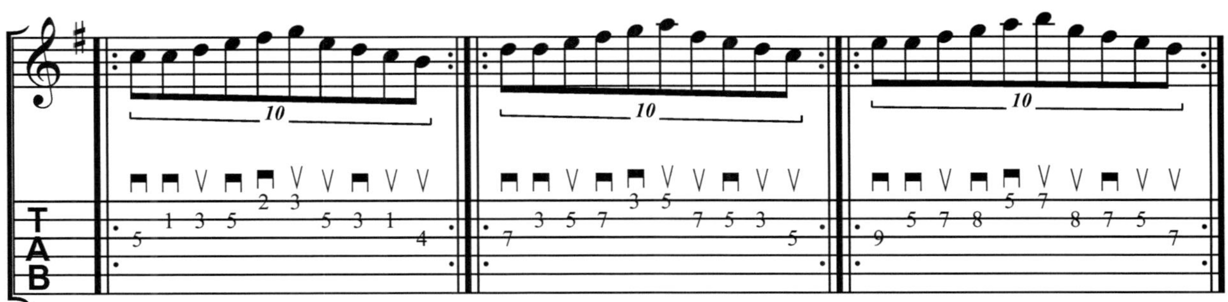

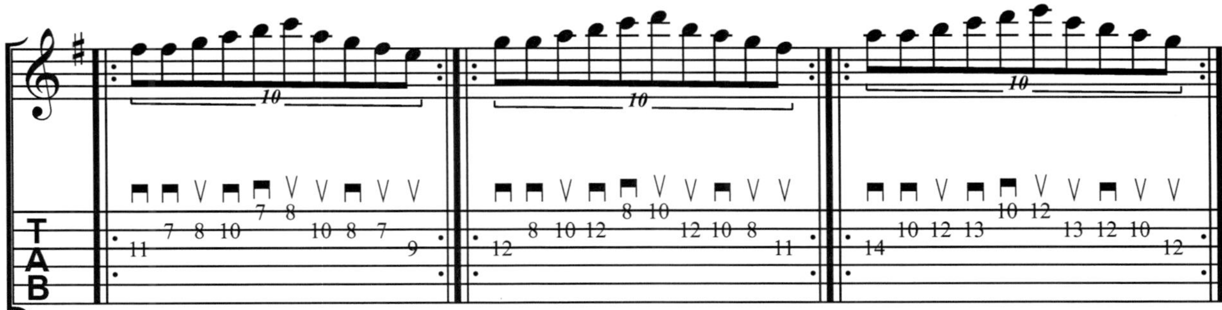

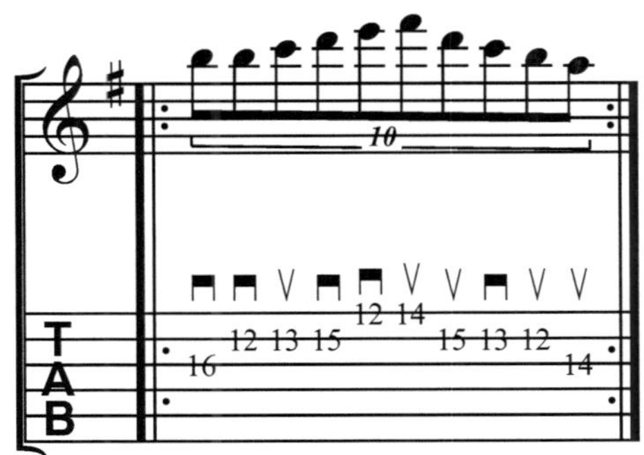

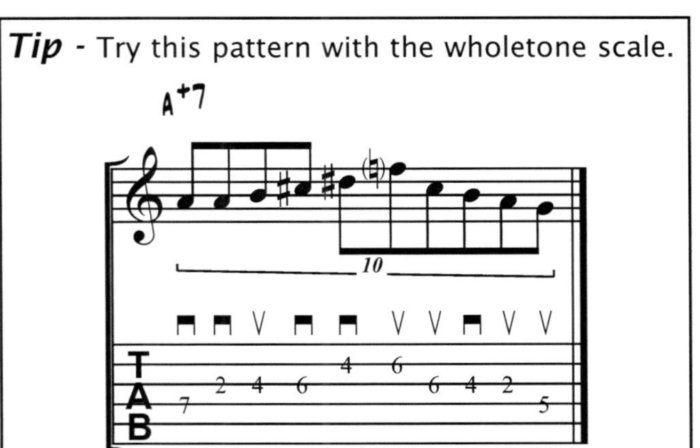

Exercise 18 - Kreutzer-Like

This pattern is inspired by the French composer / violinist, Rodolphe Kreutzer (1766–1831) It is an excellent cross-picking exercise. Though it is diatonic to G Major, experiment by utilizing wholetone, melodic minor, diminished and other scales as well.

Make sure you transpose to other string groupings too.

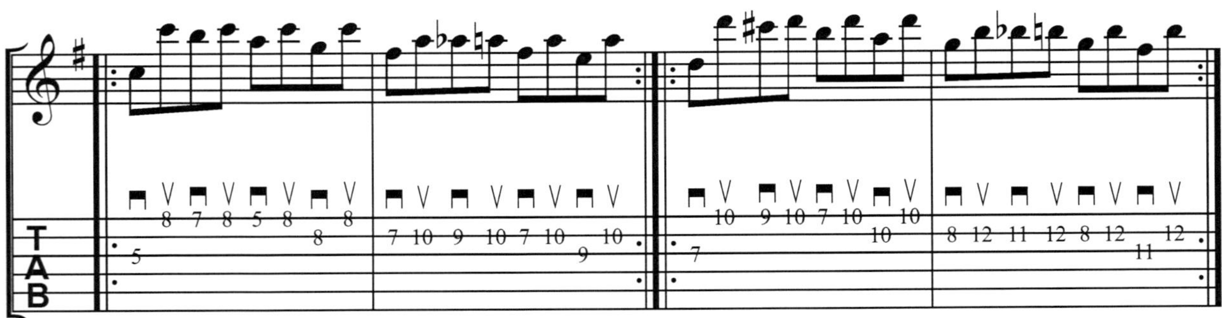

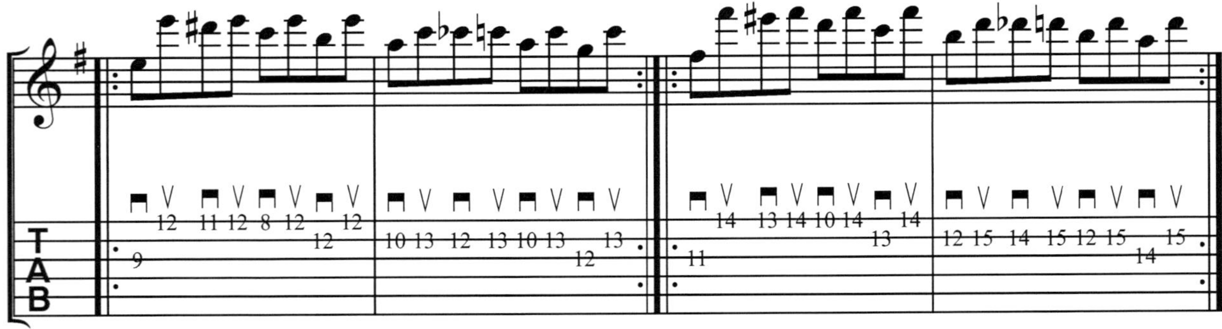

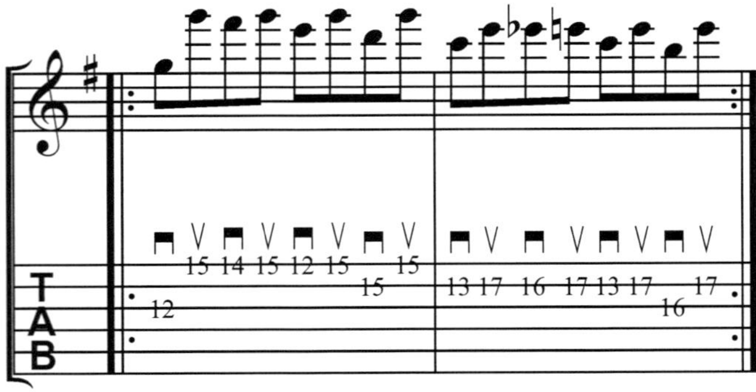

Exercise 19 - Shawn Lane inspired Diatonics

This exercise is inspired by Shawn Lane's incredibly fast and fluid odd note groupings. Shawn used to play these types of devices at lightning speed until they became just a burst of color. The first example utilizes nonuplets (groupings of 9 over 8). Like some of the other exercises of similar nature, you can ignore the polyrhyhmic aspect of this and just play the notes as a splash of musical color.

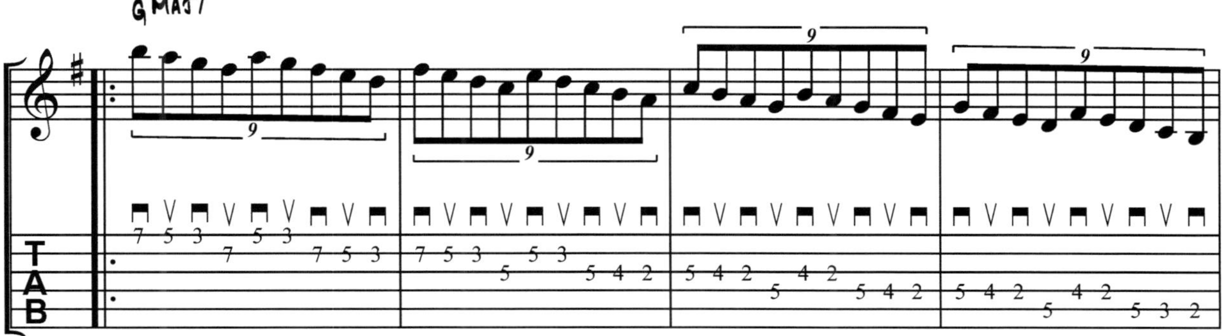

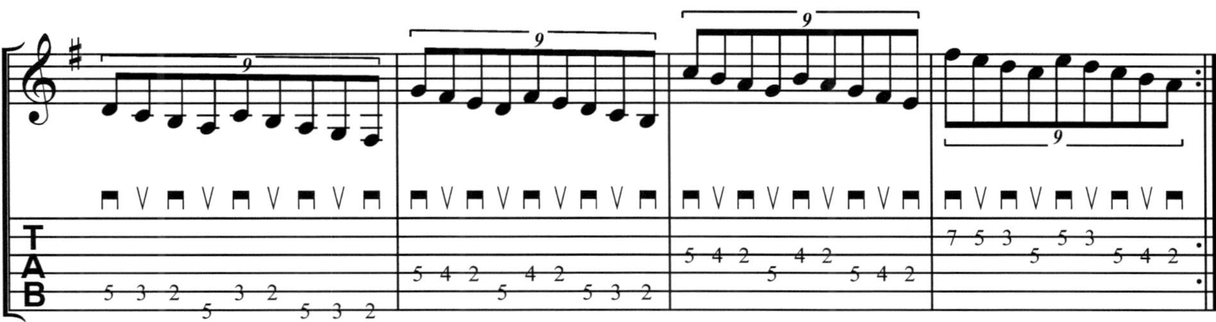

Similar exercise but in septuplets.

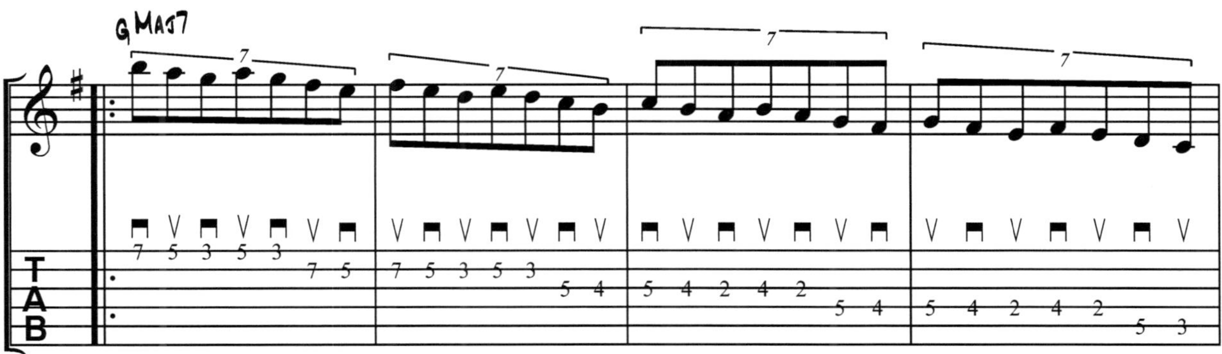

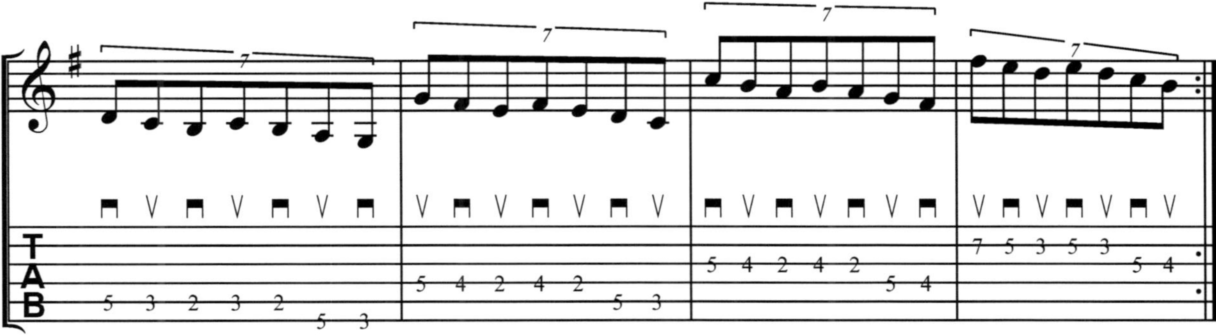

Exercise 20 - Cooleyesque Diatonic

Inspired by Speed God Rusty Cooley, this exercise is a good one for position shifting and alternate picking. It takes a simple diatonic idea and moves it up and down the neck. It can be played at very rapid speeds. It is diatonic to G major so can be used over Gmaj7, Am7, Em7, Cmaj7#11 etc.

Work this out with diminished, whole tone, melodic minor, and other tonalities.

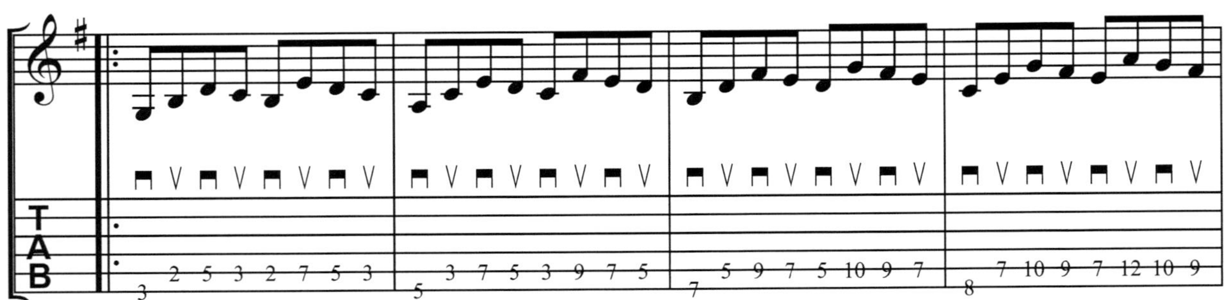

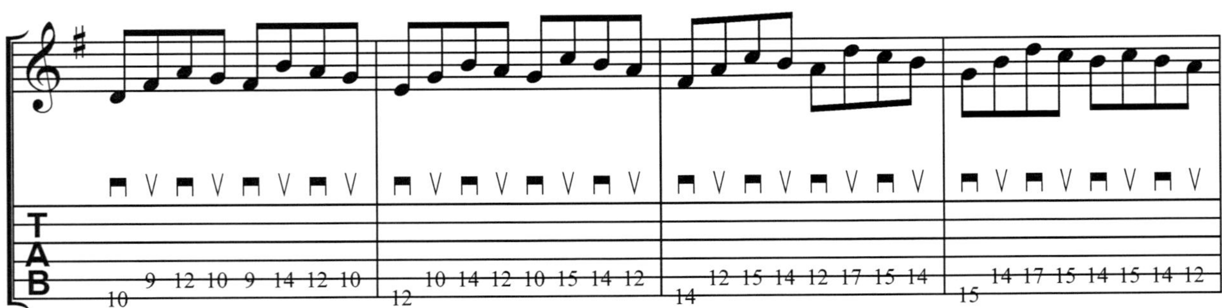

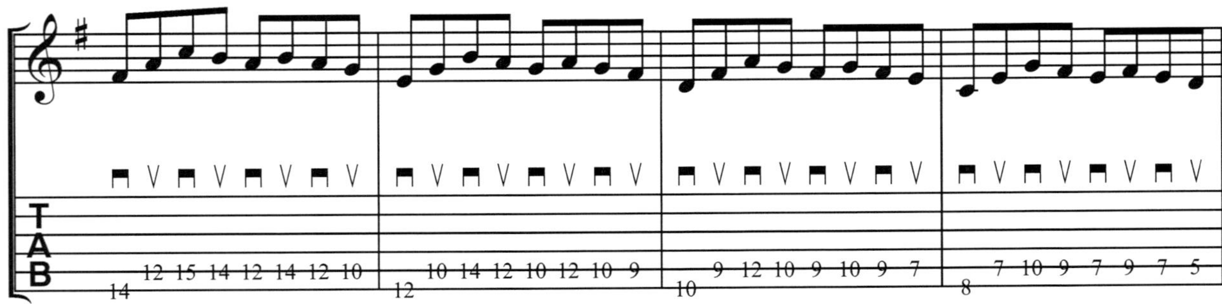

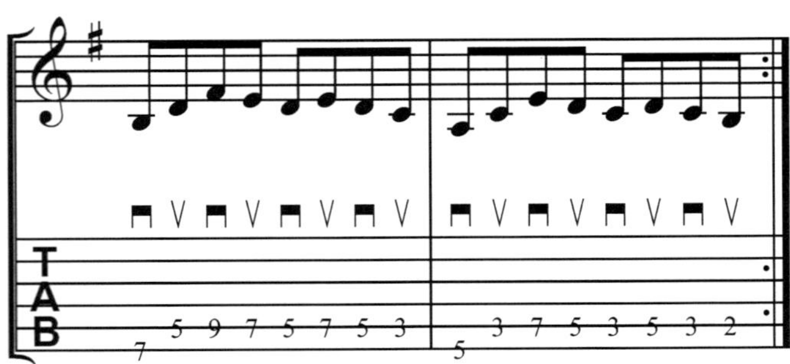

Exercise 21 - Cascade of parallel 5ths

This is an example of cascading 5ths played diatonically across the neck of the fingerboard in diatonic 4ths. It's an easy and wonderful way to incorporate modern intervals into your playing. Although it is notated over Amin7, the pattern is completely diatonic and can be played over any diatonic chord in the key of G.

The first two diatonic modes of this sequence are notated. Continue through the entire sequence...

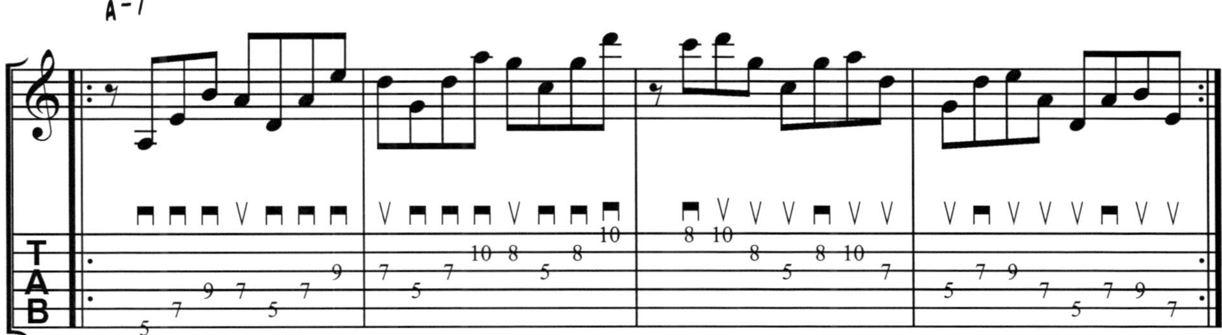

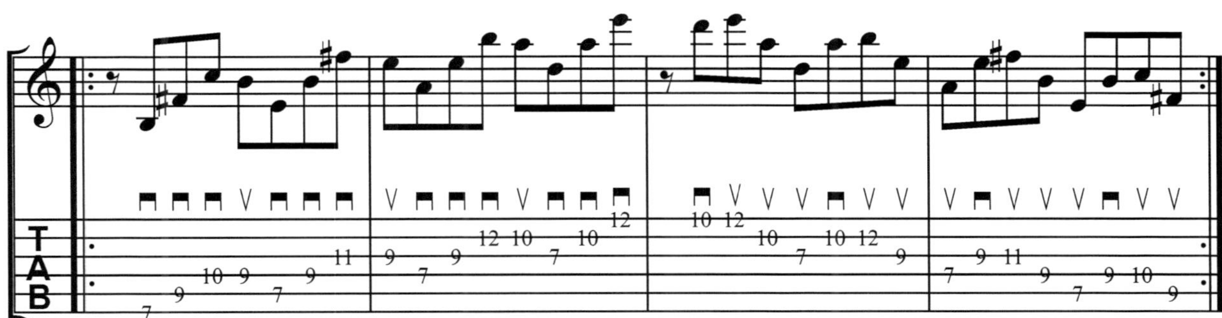

Real World Example: This example is over a ii V I chord progression. The example utilizes diatonic 4th chords in G Major over the Amin7 chord, and built on Db Major over the D7Alt chord. Notice that the 2nd chord sequence carries over into the Tonic (G Maj7) chord creating a temporary dissonance before resolving.

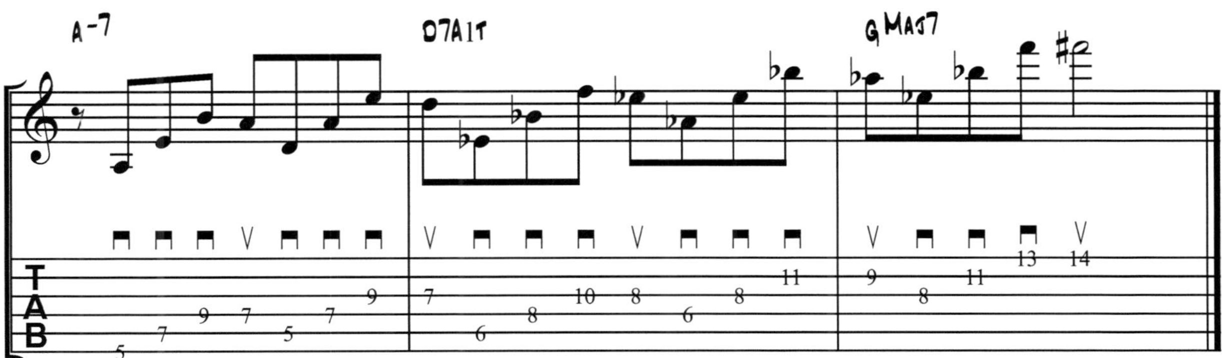

Exercise 22 - Forward momentum 4th triads

Inspired by Dan Wall by way of local phenom, Al Krasel (www.alkrasel.com), this exercise utilizes forward momentum to make a 4th chord arpeggio sound more interesting.

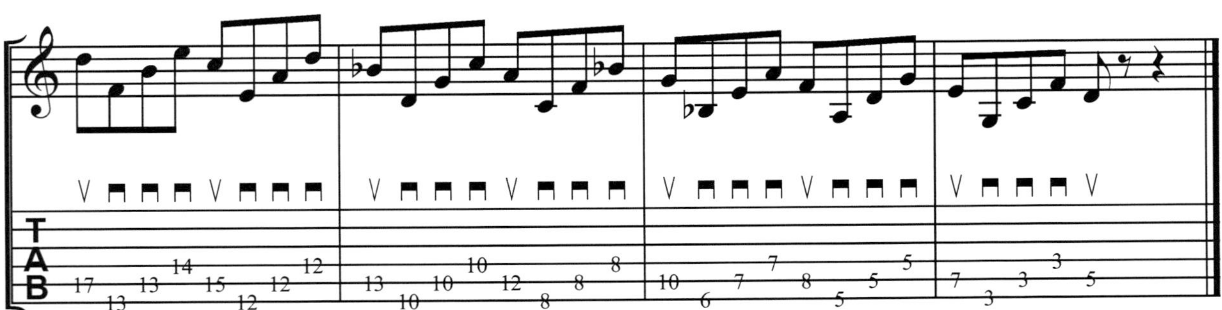

Real World Example: This example demonstrates inside outside playing using chromatic displacement over a Gm7 vamp. Note that the Abmin7 chords are indicated for analysis only. The line is meant to be played over a Gmin7 chord.

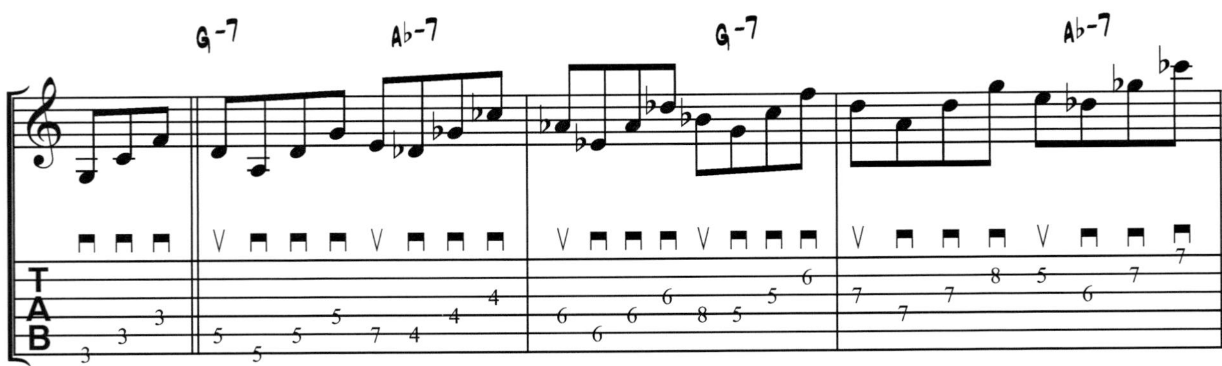

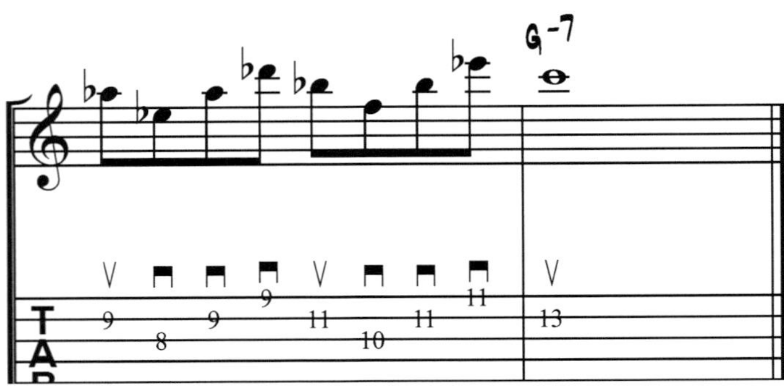

Exercise 23 - 6 String, 13th chord sweep

This is a great exercise in the Frank Gambale tradition. It's based on a 4 note rake (2nd-5th notes of each pattern) but extended throughout the range of the instrument utilizing arpeggio scale techniques. Note that these patterns generally outline a 13th chord over each fragment (minus the 11th) but you should analyze them in ways other than the chords indicated (for reference purposes)

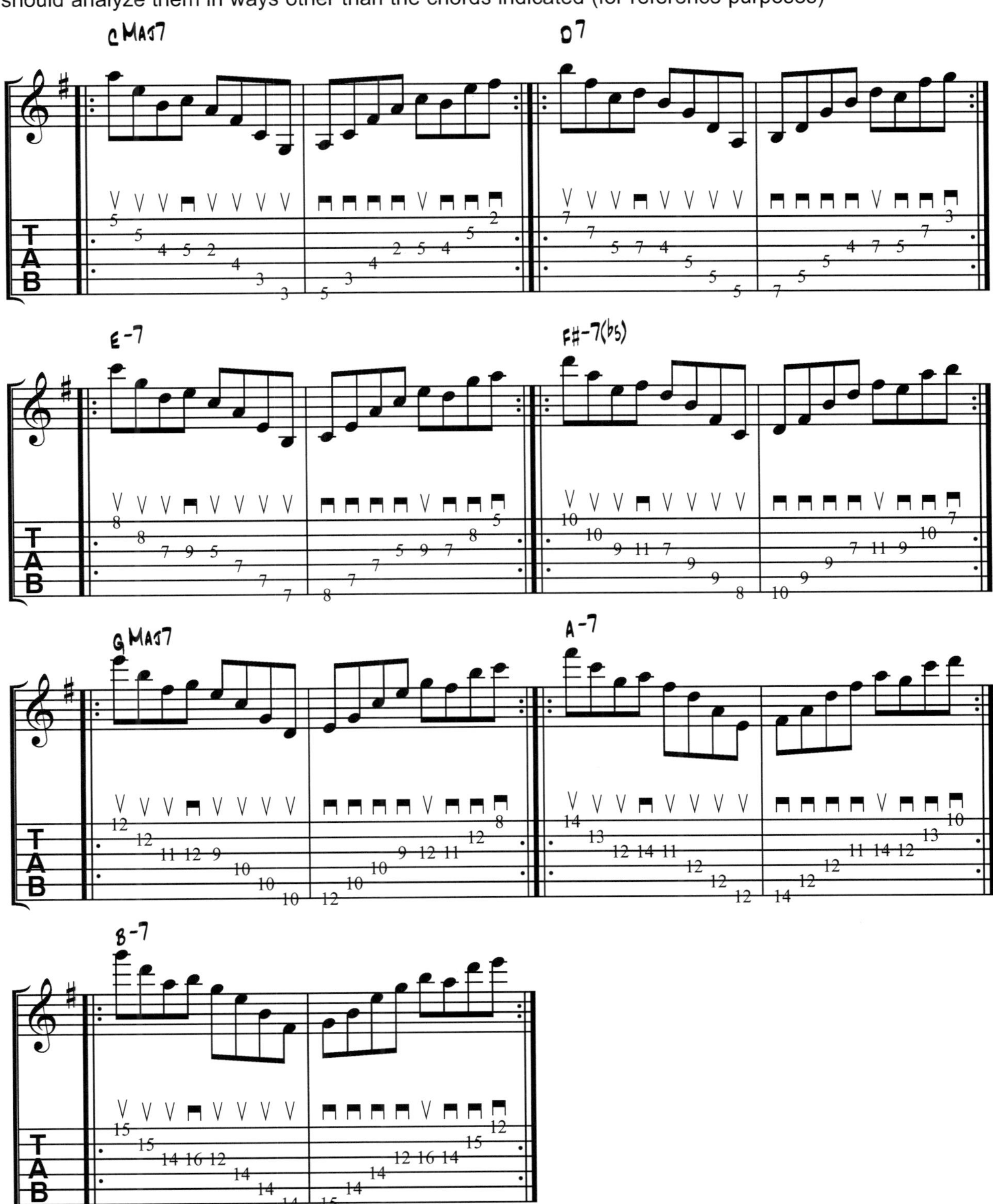

Exercise 24 - 2nd Inversion 4th Triad + diatonic

This is a pattern borrowed from the chickin' pickin' repetoire but played as a 2nd inversion 4th triad and diatonic extension.

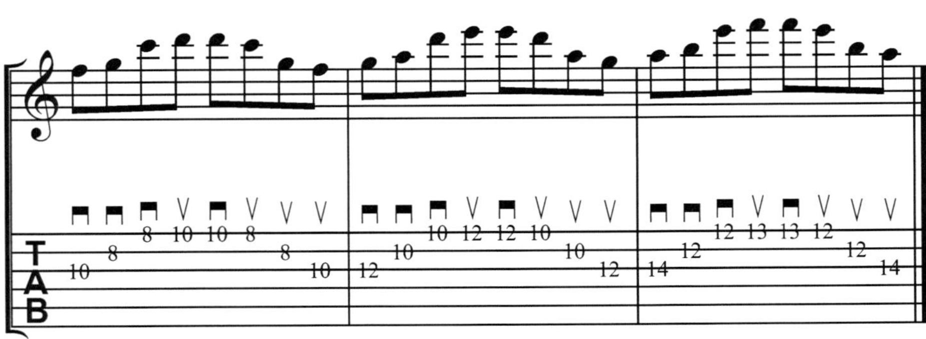

Exercise 25 - Backswept Wholetone

This exercise makes use of backsweeping. With this technique, you are not strictly sweeping since you are sometimes going against the grain in terms of string direction but each individual arpeggio is swept in the proper direction.

Soloway Swan

Exercise 26 - Miscellaneous 6 String Swept Arpeggios

This exercise consists of a bunch of miscellaneous 6 string swept arpeggios. The sky is the limit here. You can take this pattern whereever you want and over any selection of chords of note sequences your heart desires!

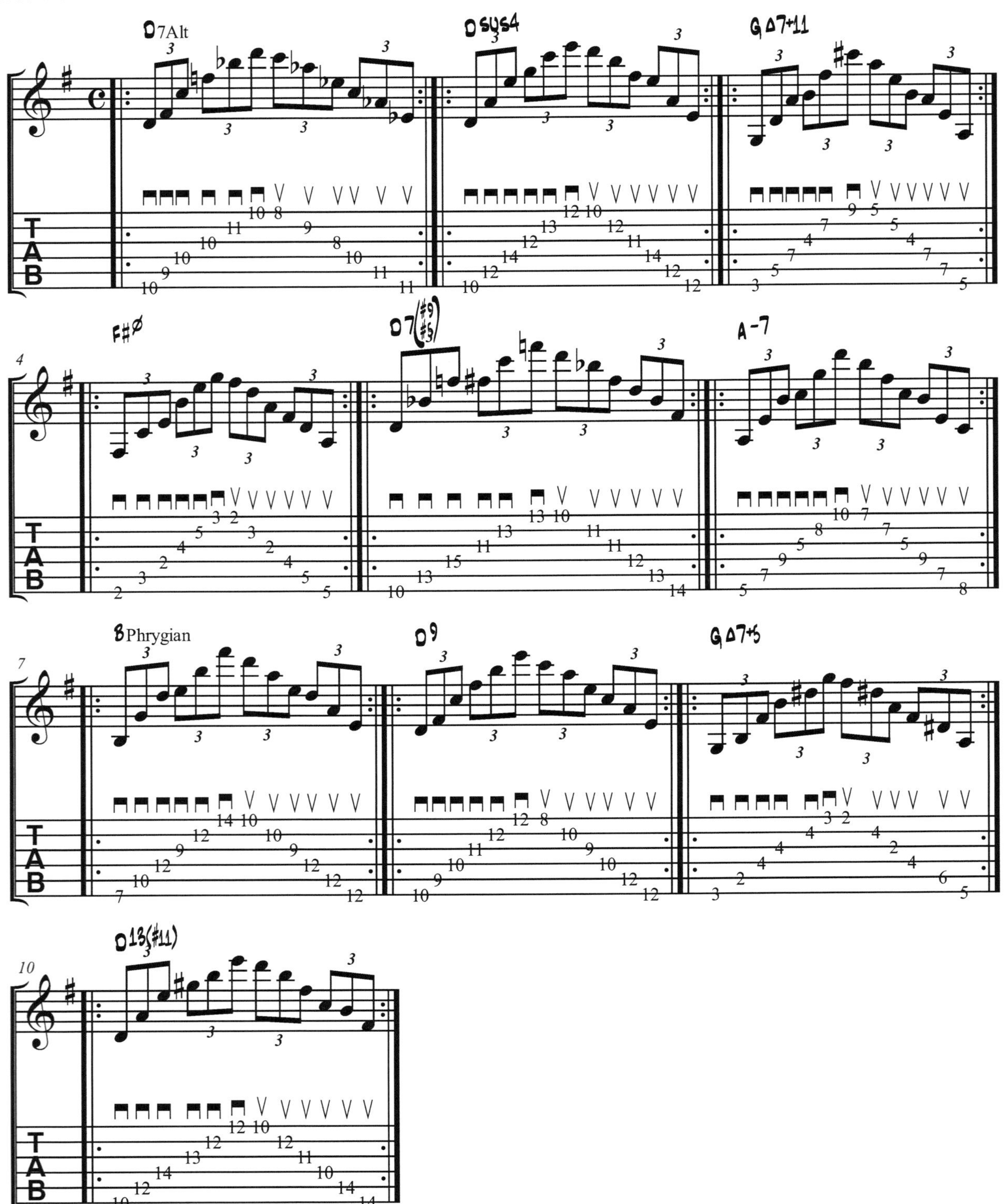

Exercise 27 - Arpeggios with Chromatic Approach

This exercise consists of an arpeggio but each note of the arpeggio is decorated by a note a 1/2 step below it. For example 1-7-1 , b3-2-b3, 5-b5-5 etc. You can either play it in triplets or as written which is a 3 over 4 feel, reminiscent of Pat Martino. It's imperative you work your way through every chord type with these arpeggios.

Here's another example. Same principal but here we're slurring every other note. This one is tricky because of the picking. The melodic line is from A Melodic minor and I've indicated it over CMaj7#5 but it could be used over A-, D7 or even G#7Alt.

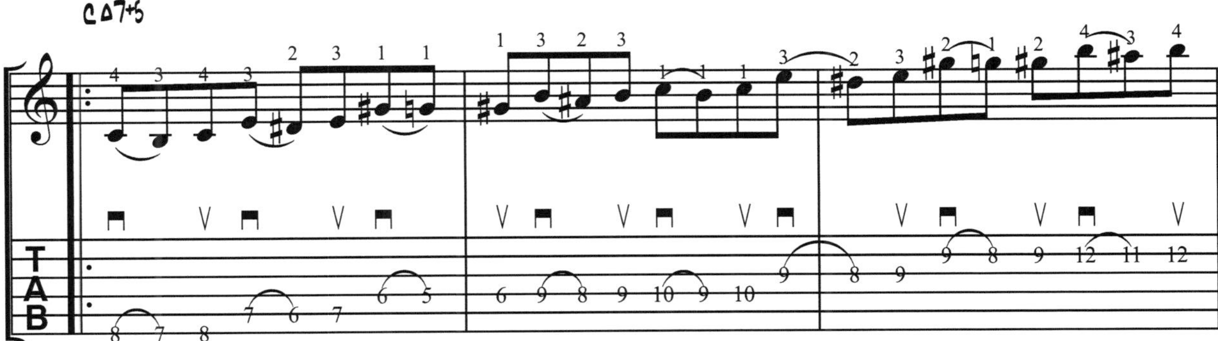

Friends

Henry Johnson - www.HenryJohnsonJazz.com

Sheryl Bailey - www.SherylBailey.com

Pentatonic Designs

Exercise 28 - 7 over 8 Pentatonic Waterfall Diatonically Extended

This is a 7 over 8 waterfall pentatonic extended in 4ths across the fingerboard. The repeated notes sound like false fingerings on the saxophone and are very Breckerish. Apply this to all pentatonic positions / modes.

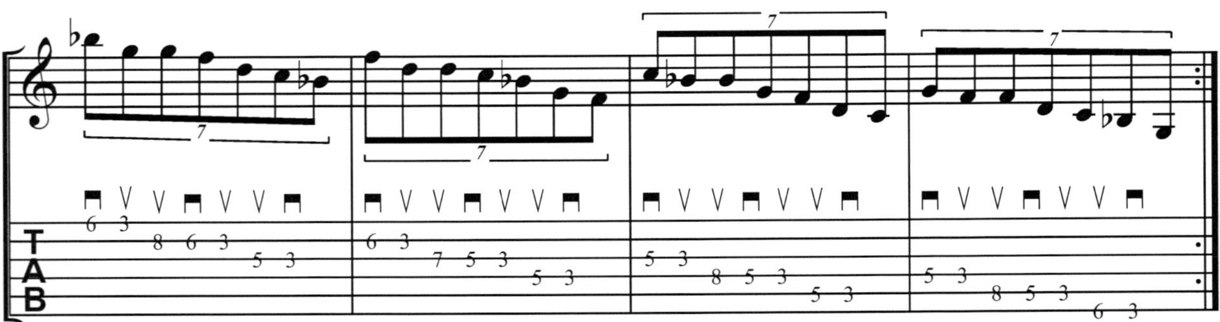

Here's a variation of the above exercise utilizing 11 over 8 and chromatic displacement to create an inside / outside feeling over the GMin7 chord. Though written in ascending form, make sure you work out the descending form as well. (The Ab-7 is for analysis only. The entire line is meant to be played over Gmin7)

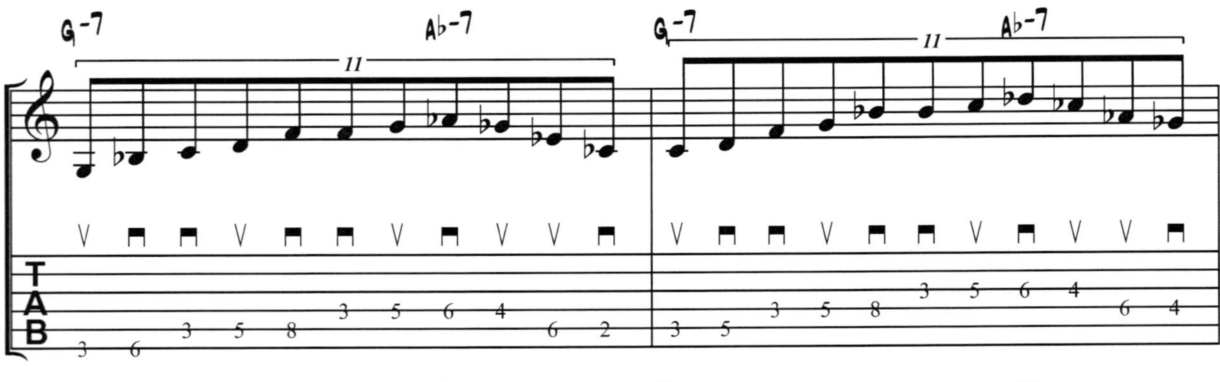

Exercise 29 - McCoy Pentatonic

This pattern is influenced by McCoy Tyner. It combines diatonic 4ths, pentatonics and sweep picking. It's very challenging and fun to play.

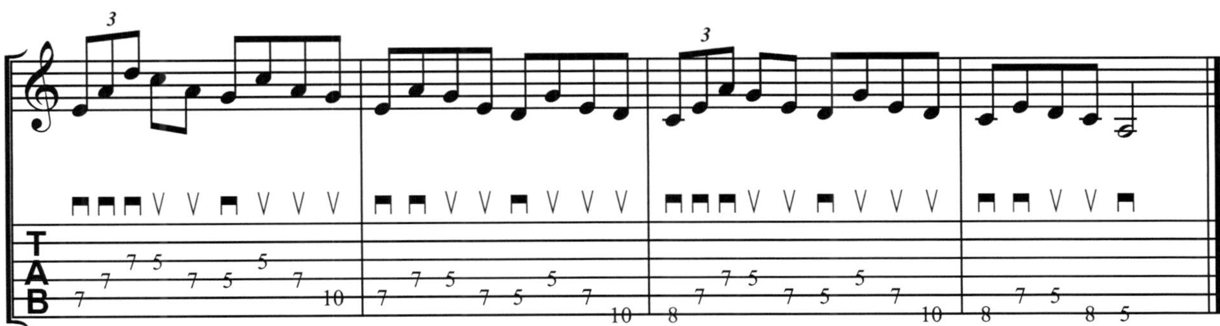

Here's the pattern in reverse:

Exercise 30 - McCoy Pentatonic with Chromatic Displacement

Here's the same pattern with *inside-outside* chromatic displacement applied. It is played over A-7. The Bb-7 is shown for for analysis purposes only.

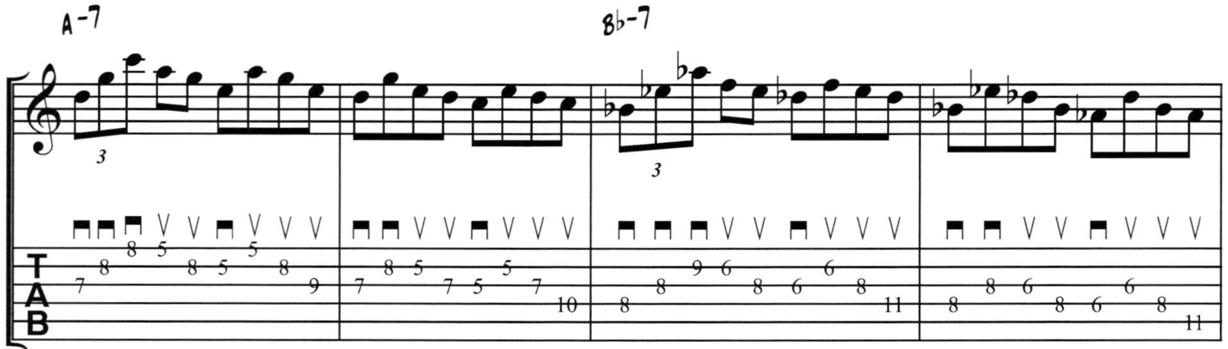

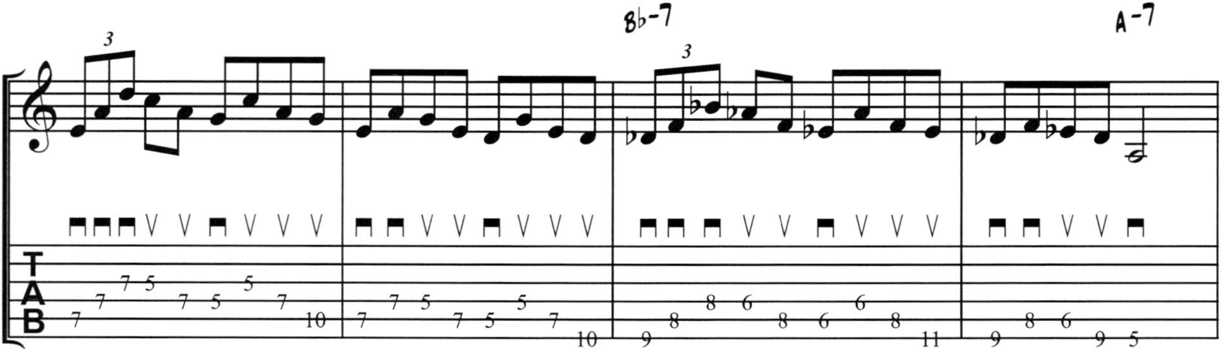

Here's the pattern in reverse:

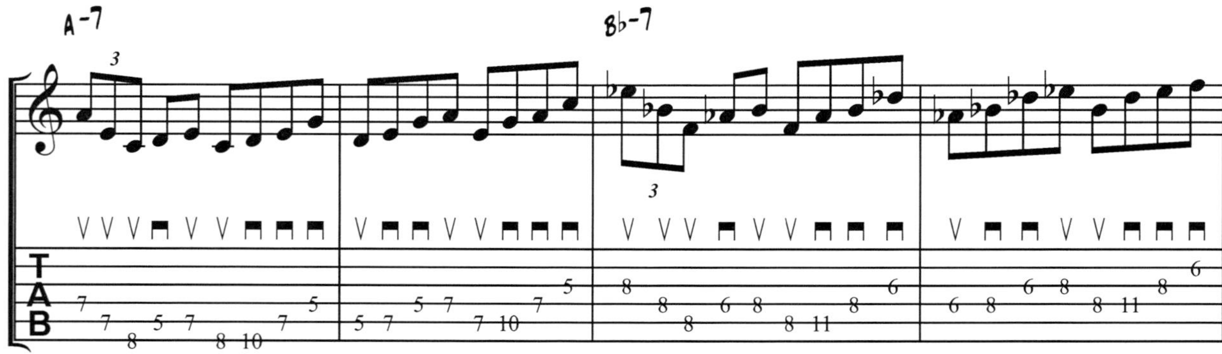

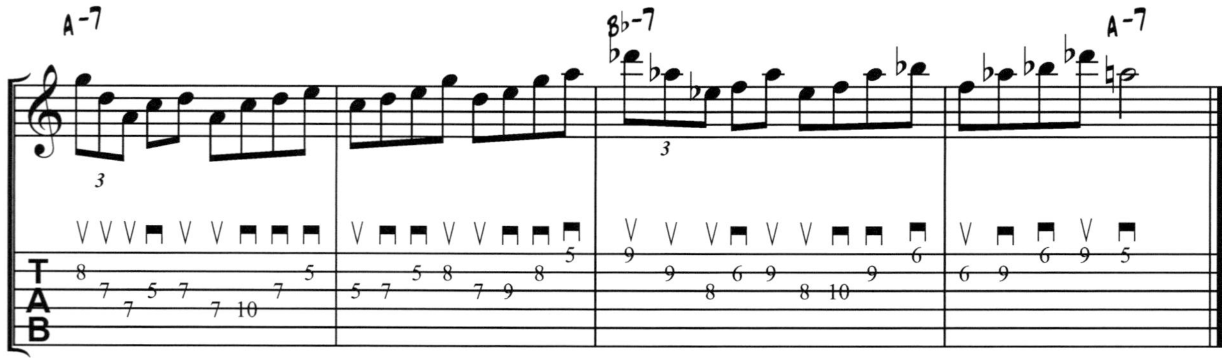

Exercise 31 - 7 over 8 Multi-Positional Pentatonic

This pattern utilizes a 7 over 8 rhythm. It may be played as a septuplet or simply as a flurry of notes. It is the most difficult pattern in the book because of the stretching and shifting required.

A shift occurs in every measure. Take this one slowly. Don't be surprised if it takes months to play cleanly. The effort is worth it.

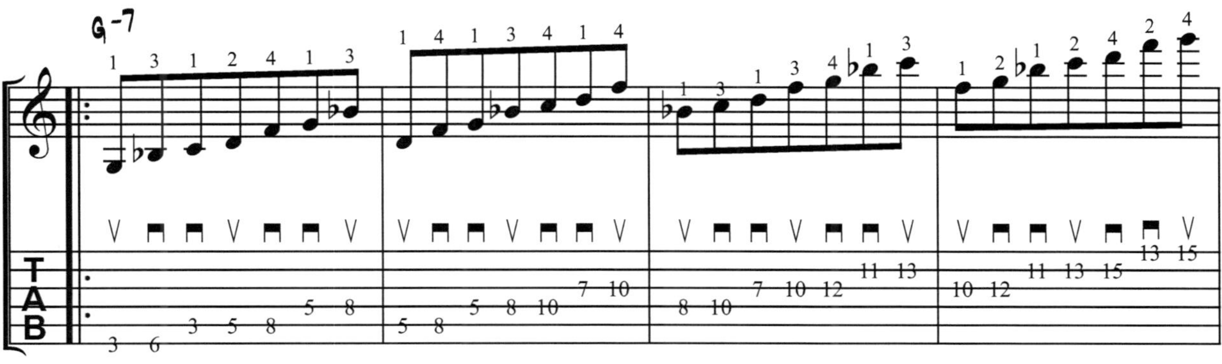

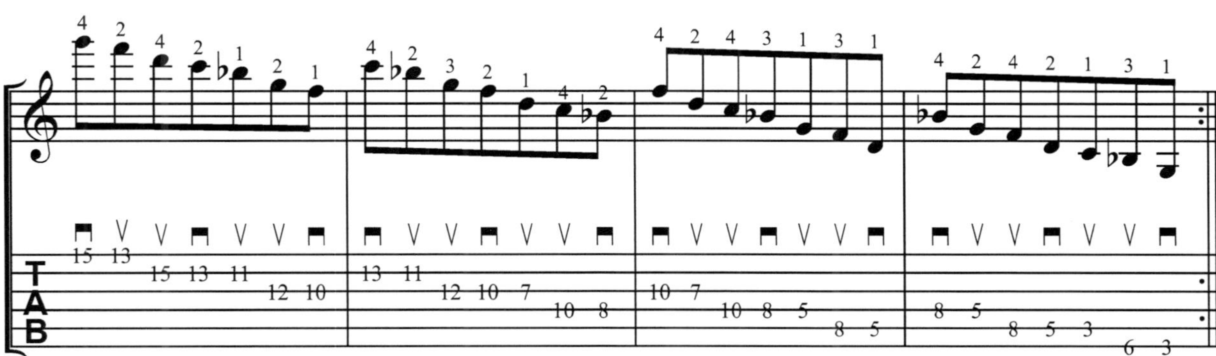

Exercise 32 - Swept Pentatonic Long Form

This is the long form of the swept pentatonic scale presented in **Sheets of Sound Vol I**. This is a really great way to play fast pentatonic scales and to get to new positions on the fingerboard. Take your time with this as it is relatively difficult to master.

Note the arrows which denote the position shifts. Only one position is written out but this pattern should be methodically worked out in all 5 positions.

Exercise 33 - 2 Position Repeated Note Pentatonic

This line sound like something Shawn Lane or Jan Hammer would have played. Relatively easy to get under the fingers and has a great percussive effect due to the repeated notes between each string change.

Exercise 34 - Shawn Lane Inspired Nontuplet Pentatonics

This is the pentatonic version of the nontuplet line presented earlier in the Diatonic chapter and presented in this chapter with pentatonics and repeated notes. Very Breckerish sounding and fun to play on guitar.

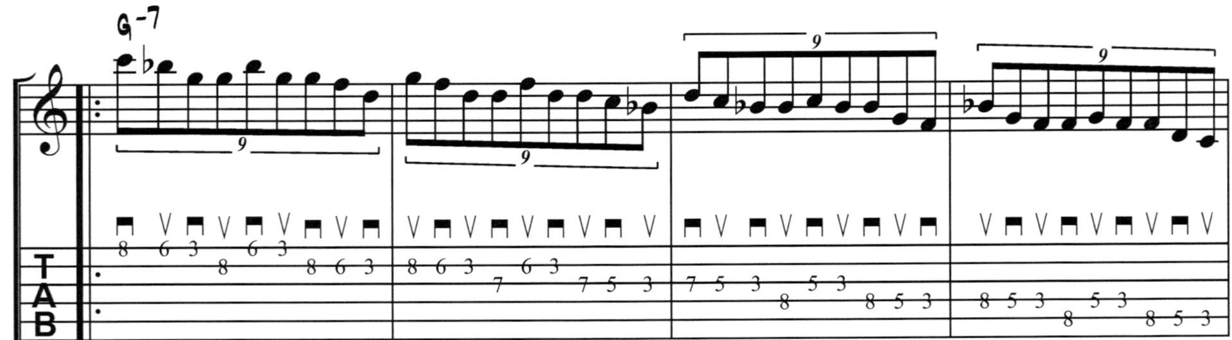

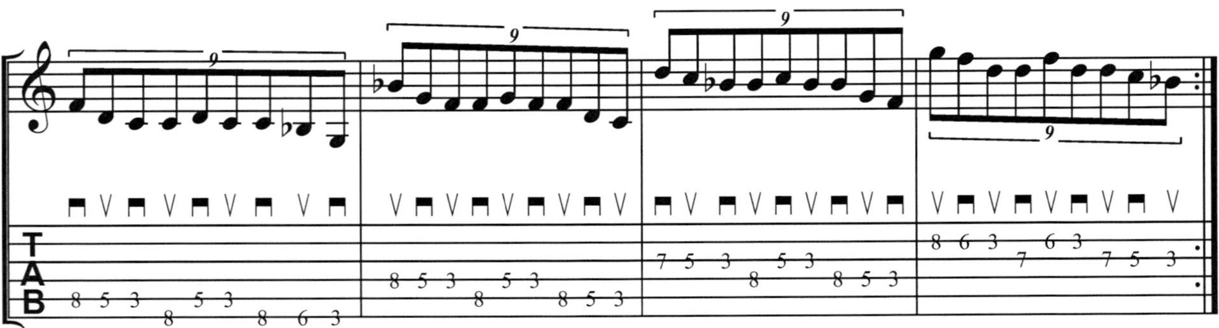

And here's the same pattern moved up the neck on a single string grouping. This covers a lot of territory very quickly. The arrows denote the position shifts (at the beginning of each measure)

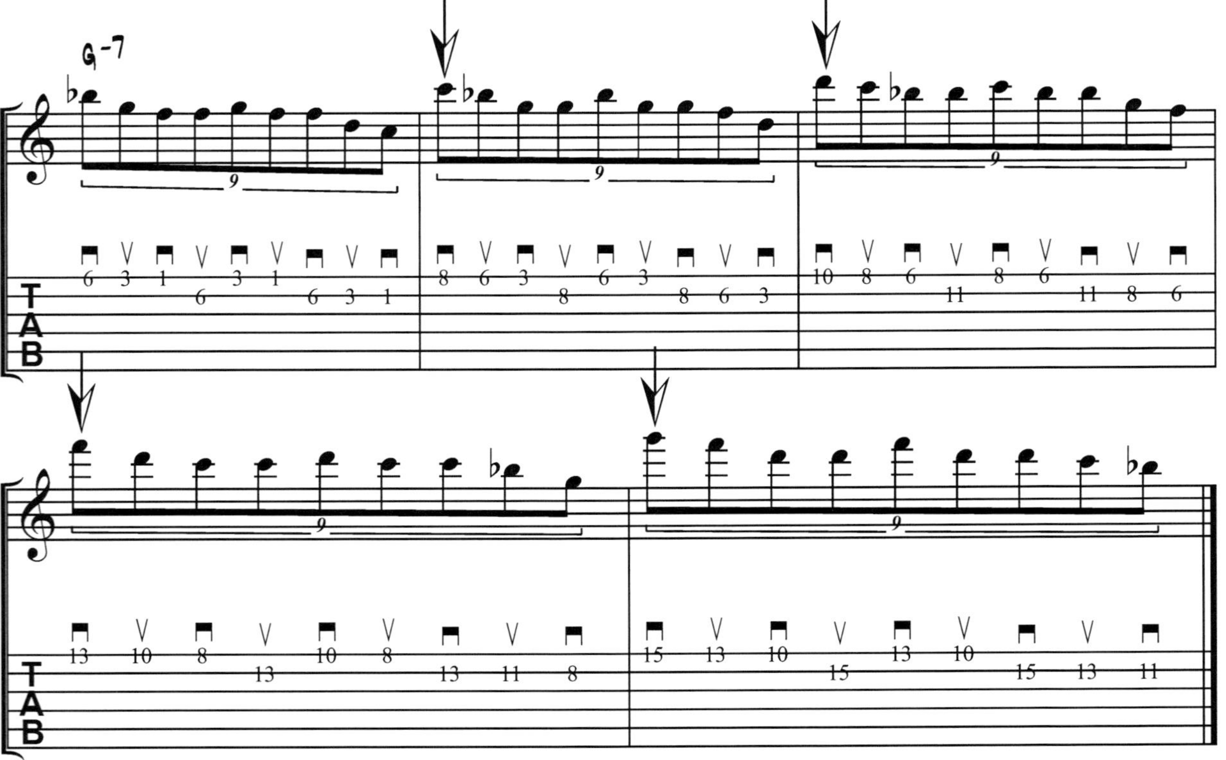

Exercise 35 - Shawn Lane Inspired Nontuplet Pentatonics, chromatically displaced

Here's the same example utilizing chromatic displacement. Note - The root chord is G-7. The Ab-7 is shown for analysis purposes only. However, you could just as easily use this line over an Ab-7 chord sequence using the G-7 as the chromatically displaced element.

Exercise 36 - Forward Motion Pentatonic 3rds

This is an interesting pattern. It consists of inversions of G pentatonic 3rds along with a pentatonic 4th. Because of the nature of the pentatonic scale, some of pentatonic 3rds end up as 4ths and some of the 4ths end up as #5 intervals.

The following are 5 inversions of the pattern moving across the fingerboard. Each pattern is 3 measures long and should be played in a new position, indicated by the roman numerals.

As is standard for G pentatonic, this line works over Gmaj, Emin7, Cmaj7, A7sus, Db7Alt, etc.

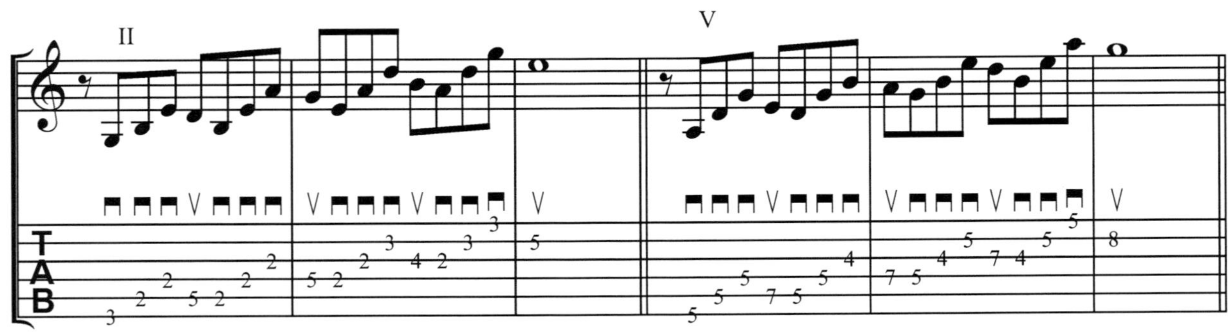

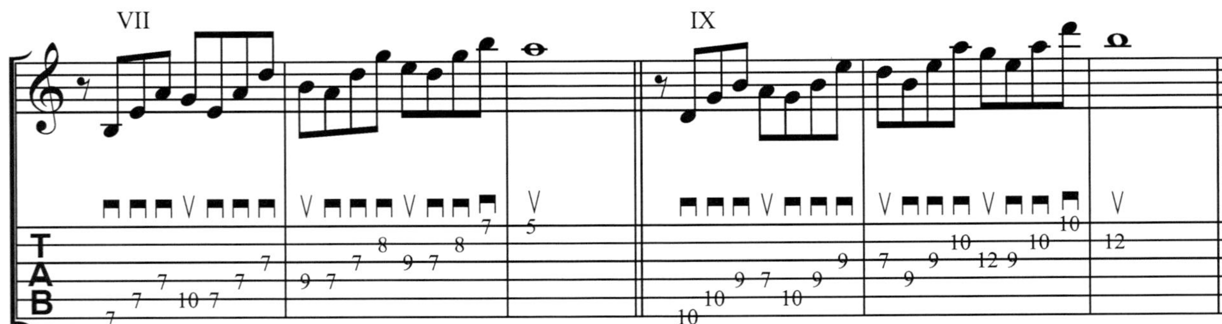

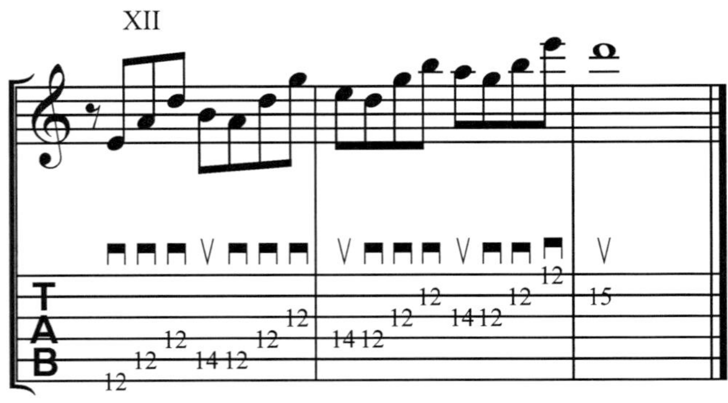

Artist's Studies

Sheets of Sound for Guitar Vol II

Exercise 37 - Pat Martino Studies

Here are a few studies in the style of Pat Martino. The first exercise is designed as an endurance test of alternate picking. I have notated it starting on an upstroke. Normally you would play something like this beginning with a downstroke but I have deliberately given this the opposite treatment. The intent is to repeat this for 1 to 2 minutes at a time at a tempo to increase the strength of your upstroke. Concentrate on making the upstrokes and downstrokes the same levels.

37.1

Note the characteristic Martino voice leading over min7 chords with the chromatic sequence between the 4th and the minor 3rd.

37.2

The next line is a very interesting one. It demonstrates a a lesser known facet of Pat's playing which makes use of sweeping.

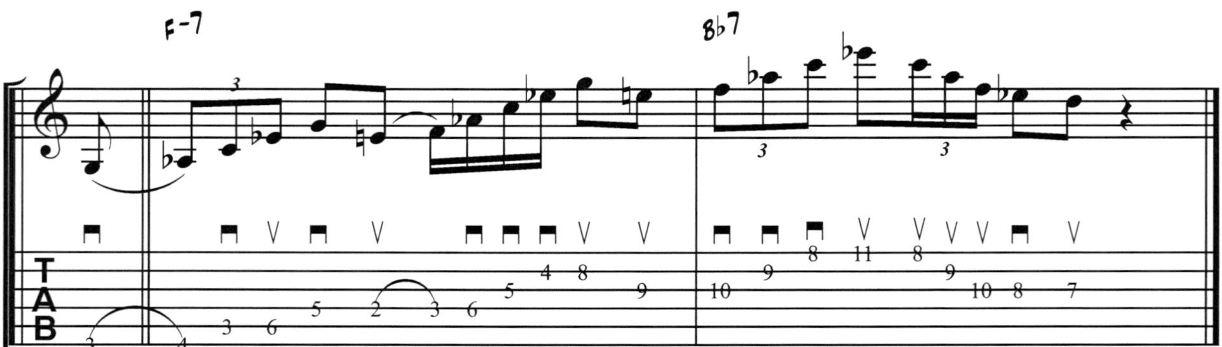

37.3

The next line is a typical Martino line with muted notes and chromatics.

Exercise 38 - Benson Studies

George Benson is the preeminent guitarist of our times. Like Wes Montgomery in the late '50s and early '60s, George is without peer in terms of blending the perfect compliment of chops, groove and articulation.

These studies are wonderful examples of picking and position shifting. To get the authentic Benson sound, make sure to pick lightly and make each note as short and stacatto as possible.

38.1

The first Benson study is affectionately known as *Lick from Hell*. Since I was a kid, this lick as long been legendary and has baffled guitarists for decades!

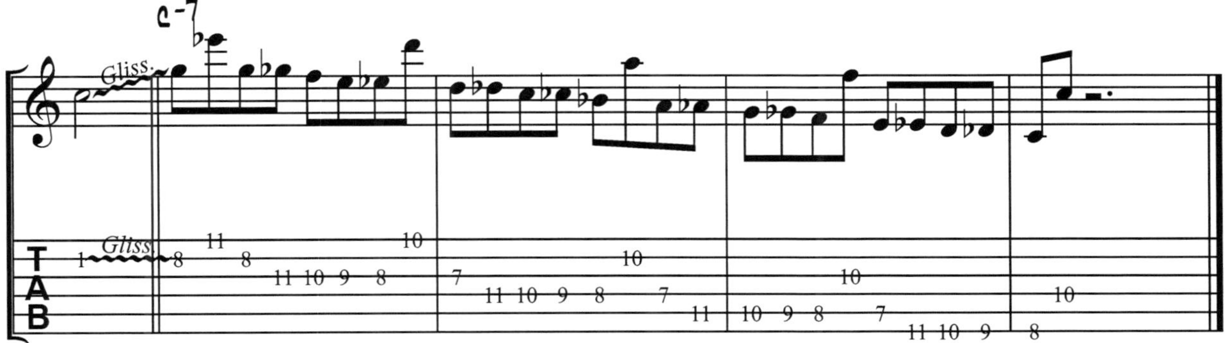

38.2

Here's another variation which is the nucleus for a set of Benson etudes

38.3

This variation stays in one position and continuously repeats. Because of the triplets, the picking gets turned around each time through the pattern. It first starts with a downstroke, then an upstroke. The arrows denote the beginning of the pattern. This is another one that should be played continuously for several minutes.

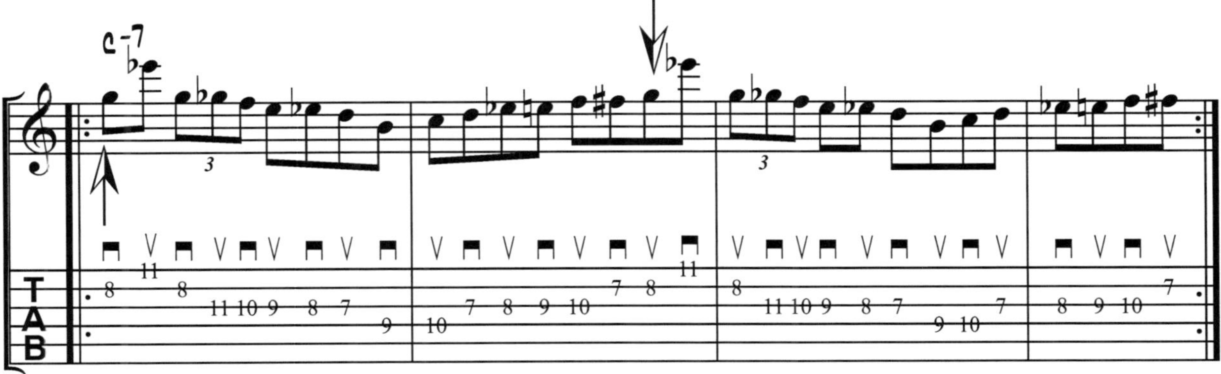

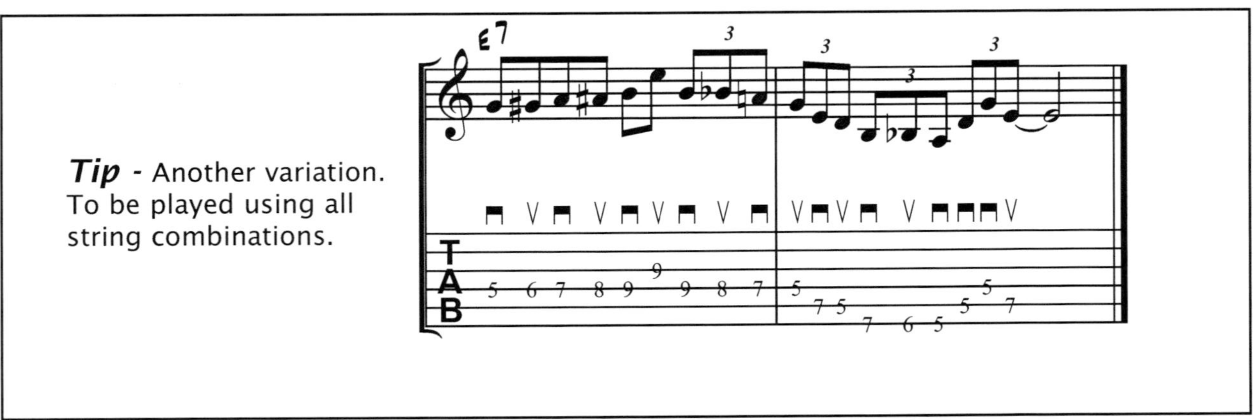

38.4

Here's a classic Benson blues lick. It's played with a bluesy, R&B feel. Note the symetrical and shifting position with a single finger during chromatic passages.

38.5

This next line was shown to me by local guitar hero, Dan Wilson. If you have not heard Dan play, do yourself a favor and check him out. You can hear him at http://www.sheetsofsound.net/danwilson.htm

38.6

This is a great positional studies based on a Benson Arpeggio/Scale (explored in more detail in the next exercise). Note the arrows which indicate position shifts.

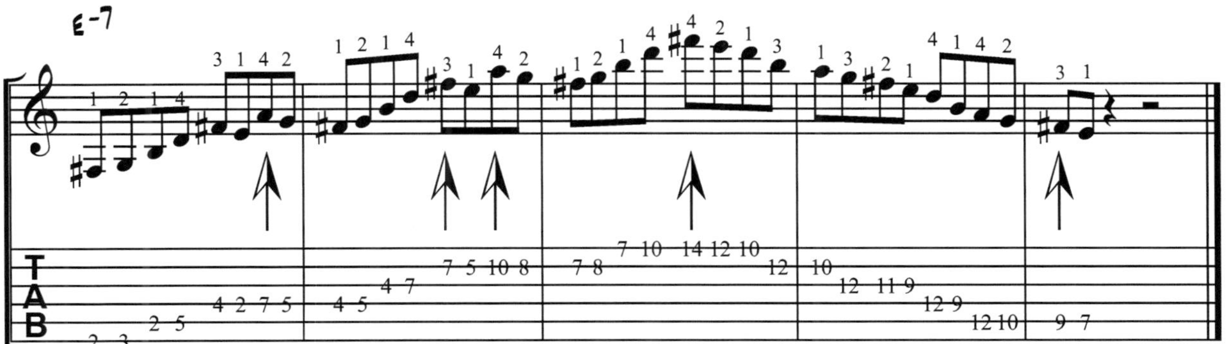

Friends

Vic Juris - www.VicJuris.com

Jimmy Bruno - www.JimmyBruno.com

Exercise 39 - Benson Arpeggio/Scale

This is a pattern utilized quite a bit by Benson for intros, cadenzas and over some of the one-chord vamps that he is famous for. It's based on a 1-2-b3-5-b7 arpeggio/scale.

Typically, these work really well when the pattern alternates between 2 notes per string and 3 notes per string although there are some exceptions.

These can also be used over the related major chords (GMaj7 or Cmaj7 with the E-7 example) or even the altered dominant (Eb7Alt with the E-7 example)

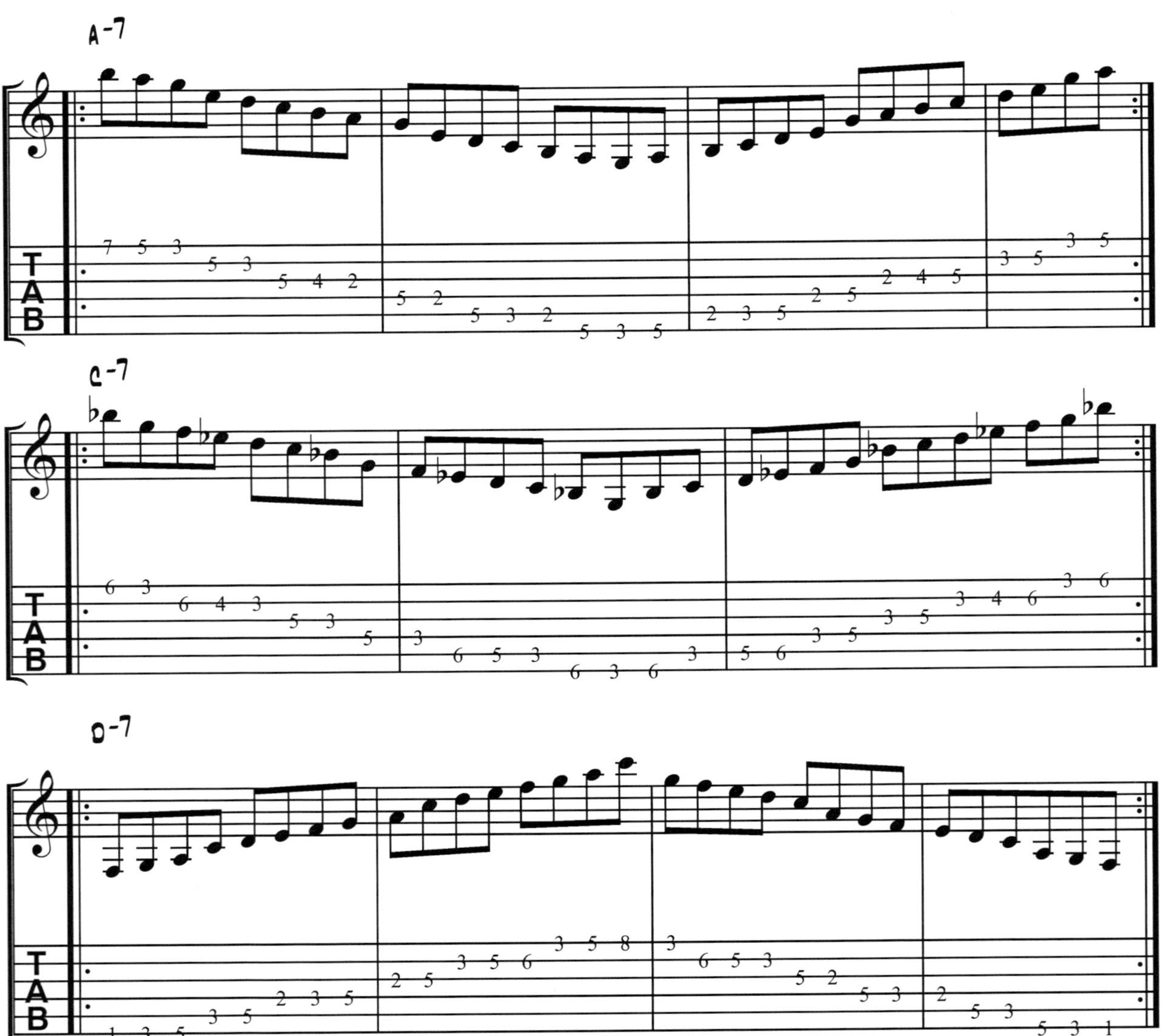

Exercise 40 - Metheny Diatonic Arpeggios Horizontal

This is a very interested and modern sounding line with a decidedly Methenyesque flavor to it. It consists of diatonic 7th chord arpeggios with a diatonic approach note. Each arpeggio is 4 notes and the entire pattern is moved across the fingerboard in diatonic 4ths. Try it with a bounce and you'll get the Metheny flavor. The indicated chords are for analysys purposes. These lines can be used diatonically over any G Ionian or related tonalities.

Exercise 41 - Gambalesque Studies

41.1

Here's a classic Frank Gambale line. Notice the rapid position shifts (indicated with arrows), and the burst of notes at the end.

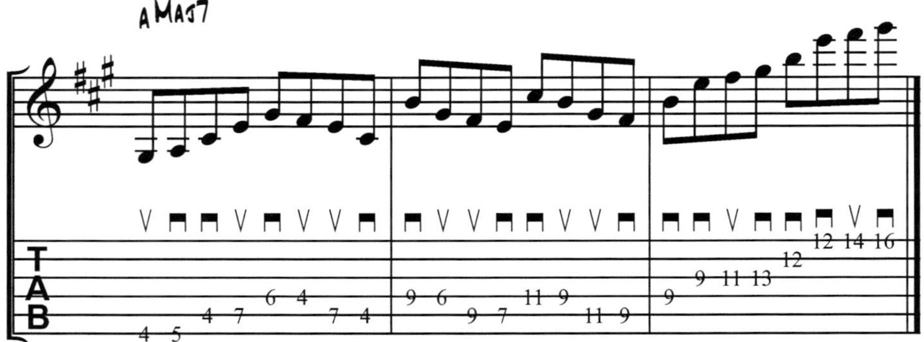

41.2

Classic Frank Gambale riff. These are raked across the strings. Note the 2 downstrokes in a row with the skipped string.

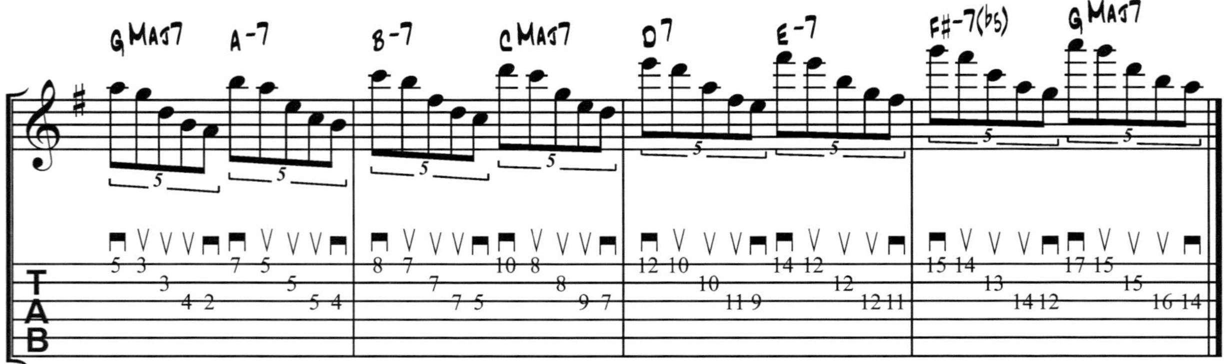

41.3

Gambale upswept arpeggios. A slight variation of the previous example.

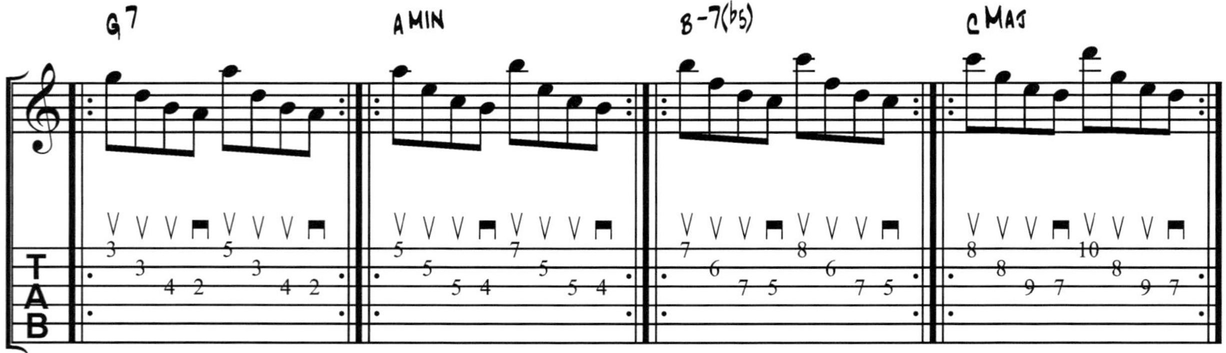

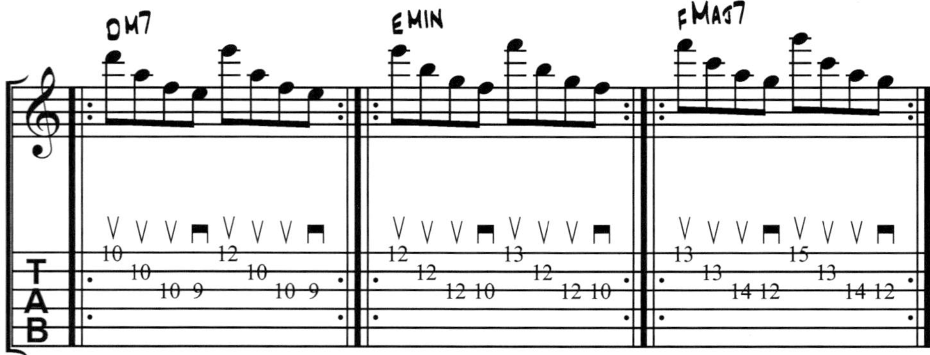

Exercise 42 - Metheny / Trane Etude

This etude is played over the famous 'Trane changes. The chords are indicated for reference.

It utilizes the well-known Pat Metheny trick of pulling off to a muted open string. This is the case for all the notes you see with the (x). In this case, it's a muted G (3rd) string. Allow the finger playing the highest note in each arpeggio to *pull-off* to the open, muted string.

Notes

Notes